Pharmacy Benefits Management

Pharmacy Benefits Management

Norrie Thomas, Lon N. Larson and Nancy N. Bell

 International Foundation of Employee Benefit Plans

The opinions expressed in this book are those of the authors.
The International Foundation of Employee Benefit Plans disclaims
responsibility for views expressed and statements made in books
published by the Foundation.

Edited by Mary E. Brennan, CEBS

Copies of this book may be obtained from:
Publications Department
International Foundation of Employee Benefit Plans
18700 West Bluemound Road
P.O. Box 69
Brookfield, Wisconsin 53008-0069
(414) 786-6710, ext. 240

Payment must accompany order.
Call (800) 466-2366 for price information.

Published in 1996 by the International Foundation of Employee Benefit Plans, Inc.
©1996 International Foundation of Employee Benefit Plans, Inc.
All rights reserved.
Library of Congress Catalog Card Number: 95-81607
ISBN 0-89154-494-1
Printed in the United States of America

1.5M-1295

*Dedicated to **William R. Gardner**, whose understanding*
of the need to combine knowledge from the fields
of pharmacy and employee benefits began the process
that resulted in this book. Bill was a pioneer in managed
care and a wonderful teacher and mentor whose
professional life exemplified a commitment to excellence.

Table of Contents

Chapter 4 ... **Formularies**

Chapter 5 ... **Drug Utilization Review (DUR)**

Chapter 6 ... **Beyond Prescription Benefits Management: The Systems Approach to Patient and Pharmaceutical Care**

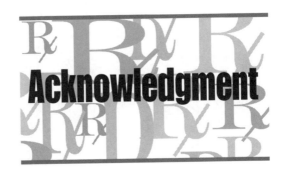

Acknowledgment

This book was supported in part
by an educational grant
from Pharmacia & Upjohn, Inc.

About the Authors

Norrie Thomas, Ph.D., is executive director, managed care, for Eli Lilly International Corp. She was formerly executive vice president, managed care, for PCS Health Systems. In 1990 Dr. Thomas founded Clinical Pharmacy Advantage, a national pharmacy benefits management company. Prior to that she was associated with PARTNERS/Aetna Health Plans, where she managed the PARTNERS pharmacy program.

Norrie Thomas, Ph.D.

Dr. Thomas, who began her career as a staff pharmacist at the Mayo Clinic, is an adjunct professor of social and administrative pharmacy at the University of Minnesota. She holds a doctorate and master's and bachelor's degrees in pharmacy from the University of Minnesota. She was previously a board member of the Academy of Managed Care Pharmacy, a national organization devoted to promoting the value of managed care pharmacists.

Lon N. Larson, Ph.D., is associate professor of social and administrative pharmacy at Drake University. He was previously a faculty member of the College of Pharmacy at the University of Arizona. Before beginning his academic career, he worked at Blue Cross and Blue Shield of Mississippi, where he was involved in systems development projects. While he was at the University of Arizona, Dr. Larson consulted extensively with the state's prepaid managed care Medicaid program.

Lon N. Larson, Ph.D.

Dr. Larson has written articles and book chapters on managed care, pharmacoecomonics and related topics. He received a B.S. in pharmacy from Drake University and an M.S. and Ph.D. in health care administration from the University of Mississippi.

Nancy N. Bell is a freelance writer and communications consultant based in Tampa. With particular expertise in health care, mental health and managed care, she writes and speaks nationally about these topics. She has authored hundreds of articles for national and regional publications, and has also written and supervised production of many marketing pieces for clients in diverse industries.

Nancy N. Bell

Ms. Bell holds an M.S. in human resources and counseling psychology from St. Thomas University in Miami and a B.A. in English from Denison University, Granville, Ohio.

Ms. Bell is the co-author of *Mental Health Benefits– A Purchaser's Guide*, also published by the International Foundation.

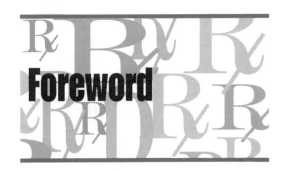

Foreword

Not too long ago, pharmacy benefits for employ-ees, when they existed at all, were a fairly small and often-overlooked part of the total health insurance package. All that has changed in recent years, as the practice of medicine and the business sides of both health care and employee benefits provision have grown rapidly and become far more complex.

Today, pharmacy benefits play a significant role in health care. In fact, they've become important enough to warrant, in many cases, widespread external management by specialized pharmacy benefits management companies (called PBMs). When drugs are prescribed and used prudently in a carefully managed environment, their potential is great for dramatically decreasing other health care expenses for everyone: payers, patients and providers.

Whether a benefits manager contracts with a PBM or handles prescription drugs in-house as part of overall health care benefits, the area has become complicated enough that a written reference on controlling the cost, quality and access of drug benefits through the art and science of pharmacy benefits management should be helpful, if not downright necessary. The majority of benefit managers are not–and should not be expected to be–experts in either the clinical or the financial aspects of prescription drugs. This book was written as a guide to the basics, the nuts and bolts of pharmacy benefits, to tell you what you need to know in language that's understandable and applicable (to the extent possible) to your own situation.

Pharmacy Benefits Management was designed primarily for benefits managers, human resource professionals and anyone else who is responsible for benefits administration. Its intent is to provide a well-organized, clear and simply written reference that deals with the most important aspects of pharmaceutical benefits. Considerable attention is devoted to the process of evaluating and selecting a PBM because so many companies are choosing to work with these specialized firms. However, the book will also provide a review of the field for pharmacists, pharmaceutical manufacturers and marketers, health plan administrators and others interested in the evolution and management of drug distribution in the United States.

This guidebook can be read from start to finish, but it's organized so that the reader can refer quickly in times of need to information on a particular issue or problem by turning to either the table of contents or the index. Key points are highlighted for easy reference, and most chapters end with a list of questions about that chapter's topic. For purchasers of pharmacy benefits management services, these questions can serve as a guide in the evaluation of PBM firms you are considering hiring. For others, they may be helpful as a review of the chapter's main points.

Please note that the terms *pharmacy benefits manager* and *PBM* are used to refer to whoever is managing the pharmacy benefits—whether that's you from within your company or a specialized firm with whom you've contracted. As Chapter 8 discusses in detail, many employers today are choosing to hire pharmacy benefits management *companies*, so the term most often will refer to these external managers.

There is a glossary at the back of this guidebook. You should review these terms and their definitions before reading all or parts of the text in order to familiarize yourself with the terminology, concepts and developments you'll be reading about. We hope this guidebook will provide you with exactly the information you need to make the administration of pharmacy benefits easier and more cost-effective.

Pharmaceutical benefits are quickly becoming one of the most challenging areas with which benefits managers must deal. As you've probably already noticed, managing drug benefits today involves juggling cost, quality and employee satisfaction. Finding effective ways to cut costs–or at least hold the line on price increases–is critical. Yet you must also ensure the high caliber of the pharmaceutical services provided to your employees *and* simultaneously attempt to see that covered members are satisfied with their benefits.

These days, a benefits manager must wear many hats, often acting as a purchasing specialist, health adviser, financial analyst, counselor and salesperson. At the same time, the increasing complexity of managed care requires that you be knowledgeable (at least to some extent) about the prescription drugs you are enabling your employees to obtain and the way these pharmaceutical benefits are being financed and managed.

Chapter 1...

Managing Pharmacy Benefits

Prescription benefits are no longer just a line item in the benefits budget. They are an increasingly important part of both health care and an employee's insurance package. In fact, drug benefits were somewhat responsible for the fact that 1994 marked the first decline in health care spending by American businesses in two decades. Spending fell 1.1%–not a big drop, but a significant step in the nation's ongoing struggle to contain medical costs. According to Foster Higgins, an international benefits consulting firm, the increase in companies' use of separate prescription drug plans contributed to this welcome news. Managed health care plan enrollment overall went from

52% of the workforce in 1993 to 63% in 1994. The use of managed drug benefits more than doubled in 1994. Close to half of large employers (500 or more employees) offered a prescription drug plan. The average cost was $405 per employee (up from $365 in 1993) and $595 per retiree.[1]

An increase in separate prescription benefit plans contributed to the first decline in health care spending in two decades.

According to the Marion Merrell Dow, *Managed Care Digest/ HMO Edition, 1994*,[2] 91% of all HMO members were covered for prescription benefits in 1993. Nearly all HMOs (99%) offered prescription benefits to members, almost the same as 1992. About 16% of HMOs imposed a separate deductible for pharmacy benefits. The average annual deductible was $73 for individuals and $156 for family policies.

A Brief History of Prescription Drug Benefits

At one time, just a few decades ago, the typical health insurance policy did not include prescription drug benefits. For a variety of reasons, drugs were considered a peripheral part of treating an illness, injury or chronic condition, not an integral component in the treatment continuum, as is beginning to be the case today.

American labor unions pushed for the inclusion of drug benefits in insurance coverage in the 1970s, and employers were forced to comply. At that time, however, health care costs in general were far lower than they are today, with prescription benefits accounting for only 2% to 3% of the benefit dollar.[3]

Historically, the earliest drug benefit was part of the major medical policy, with coverage effective after an annual deductible had been met. To receive reimbursement, a plan member submitted receipts from the pharmacy for the charges incurred. The contract usually required that the drug be approved by the U.S. Food and Drug Administration (FDA), that it be available by prescription only, and that it be prescribed by a physician or other approved professional for the treatment of a medical condition. In reality, the claims submitted often consisted of just a receipt from the pharmacy with the prescription number and the amount paid.

A revolution of sorts occurred in the 1980s when more sophisticated computer networks with real-time, online access to information made it possible right at the point of sale for pharmacists to check a patient's eligibility for benefits and the extent of insurance coverage. Pharmacists could also verify product cost and copayment information. By then, prescription drug benefits had risen to 7% to 10% of the health care benefit dollar, and employers were becoming more concerned about their cost.

A 1990 survey of *Business & Health* magazine subscribers found that nearly 65% of corporate executives were "concerned" or "very concerned" about the cost of prescription drugs available through their health plan; 39% said they were "aware" or "very aware" of changes in the cost of drugs; and 62% said they were paying more attention to the types of prescription drugs available through their plans.[4]

> *The appropriate use of pharmaceuticals as part of overall health care can have numerous advantages for everyone.*

The Value of Pharmacy Benefits

Drugs, and prescription drug benefits, have come a long way. Almost everyone now recognizes that the appropriate use of pharmaceuticals as part of the overall health care of individuals (and groups of employees) can have numerous advantages for everyone. As one component in a health insurance package, a comprehensive, carefully designed drug benefit should result in the following advantages:

- Fewer hospital admissions
- Shorter hospital stays
- Prevention of disease
- Less need for more expensive, invasive and unpleasant therapies, such as surgery
- Promotion of employee productivity and wellness (physical and mental)
- Longer lives
- Improved quality of life.

Drugs are so widely used because they offer significant benefits in patient treatment for a vast variety of health problems. Antibiotics, antidepressants, vaccines, antihypertensives and antiulcer agents are just a few of the drug classes that have reduced health care costs by decreasing the need for other medical or mental health services. Many diseases can now be cured (such as infections), alleviated or controlled (such as arthritis, high blood pressure, high cholesterol levels and depression), and prevented (such as heart attacks and strokes) with the appropriate use of certain drugs.

Pharmaceuticals have been largely responsible for the prevention, control or cure of many formerly deadly diseases. In 1920, for instance, the eight most serious disease groups were: tuberculosis, influenza and pneumonia, nephritis and renal sclerosis (kidney disease), intestinal illnesses, syphilis, diphtheria, whooping cough, and measles. In six of these eight categories, new drugs provided either the cure or the means of prevention. By 1965, a new group of more complex killer diseases predominated: heart disease, cancer, stroke, influenza and pneumonia, early infancy diseases, and arteriosclerosis. Again, drugs have played a central role in reducing mortality and improving quality of life for those afflicted with these illnesses.[5]

Study after study has shown that drug therapy is often the least expensive course of treatment.

Drugs Save Money

Though drugs might seem costly on an individual basis, study after study has shown that drug therapy is often the least expensive course of treatment. Ulcer drugs provide a good example. According to the Pharmaceutical Research and Manufacturers of America (PhRMA), in 1976, before modern antiulcer drugs called H-2 antagonists were developed, 155,000 ulcer surgeries were performed. By 1987, that number had dropped to under 19,000. Quick healing ulcer drugs cost about $1,000 a year, far less than surgery at a cost of approximately $25,000 per operation. The PhRMA estimates that ulcer drugs save an estimated $3 billion annually. A Medicaid study in Michigan[6] indicated that since H-2 antagonists were introduced, the number of ulcer surgeries has fallen by 88%. Recent news that many ulcers are caused by bacteria and can be cured with antibiotics will result in even more dramatic findings once studies are done.

In another example of the economic advantages of drug therapy, it's estimated that gallstone surgery costs about $12,000. Treatment with ursodiol, a drug that dissolves gallstones, costs about $1,960 per year (if treatment is required that long) and could save $2 billion annually. The potential for increased employee productivity with drug therapy versus surgery is important because patients recovering from gallbladder operations lose ten million workdays a year.[7]

In 1960 there were 55,500 new cases and 11,020 deaths from tuberculosis. In 1990, more than 25,000 cases were reported, but only 1,800 deaths, a drop of 84%, thanks to antibiotics. Before these drugs were developed, a typical TB patient spent three or four years in a sanitarium and had a 30% to 50% chance of dying. Today, with antibiotic treatment, a patient is likely to recover in six to 12 months.[8]

Schizophrenia, one of the most devastating and expensive mental illnesses, accounted for the majority of mental hospital patients until the late 1950s. In fact, most schizophrenic patients were institutionalized for much of their adult lives. The first major antipsychotic drug, Thorazine, was introduced in the mid-1950s and was followed by other "miracle" drugs for mental illness. Nearly 80% of patients using these drugs improve. By the late 1980s, 95% of patients were being treated on an outpatient basis and, with the development of Clozapine in the 1980s, many schizophrenic patients were able to work and lead productive lives for the first time.[9]

According to a 1991 PhRMA study:[10]

◑ Antibiotics have helped avoid between 60,000 and 90,000 deaths from tuberculosis during the past half century, saving $7.5 billion to $11 billion in productivity losses because of premature death and disability.

◑ Drug treatment saved 671,000 lives from heart disease and $84 billion in productivity losses between 1968 and 1986.

◑ Drugs helped prevent 500,000 stroke deaths between 1970 and 1986 at a savings of $16 billion.

◑ A year of drug therapy for angina pectoris, a heart condition, costs about $1,000, versus coronary bypass surgery at $41,000 per operation.

Similarly, new drugs for migraine headaches have been shown to substantially decrease pain and lost workdays, keeping employees on the job, where they are happier, healthier and more productive.

Drugs Cost Money

Many people think that drugs are responsible for a large part of skyrocketing health care costs. According to a 1992 Gallup Poll, consumers believed that 37% of the health care dollar was spent on pharmaceuticals; health care providers thought it was closer to 22%; and financial analysts estimated the drug cost component at 12%.[11] However, the majority of studies show that prescription drugs currently represent somewhere between 7% and 10% of health care costs. Almost $0.60 of every health care dollar goes toward hospital care and physician services, not pharmaceuticals.[12]

The following chart shows results of a 1993 survey conducted by the International Foundation of Employee Benefit Plans.[13] Benefits managers were asked what percentage of their total health care costs they spent on pharmaceuticals.

Actually, the amount of money spent on drugs is one area in which the United States compares favorably with other nations. Per capita costs

PRESCRIPTION DRUG BENEFIT COSTS
AS A PERCENT OF TOTAL HEALTH CARE EXPENSE

Drug Costs	Respondents
Less than 5%	7%
6-10%	38
11-15%	16
16-20%	4
21-25%	3
More than 25%	1
Don't know	31

for pharmaceuticals are higher in England, Japan, Germany, France, Canada and Australia than they are here.[14]

Benefits managers have seen the cost of drug benefits increase between 15% and 20% annually over the past five years.[15] In the second half of 1991, the Group Health Association of America (GHAA) reported that HMOs they surveyed reported individual drug price increases of as much as 1,000%. Their expenditures for outpatient pharmaceuticals overall rose 17% to $109.43 per member per year in 1993, up from $93.57 in 1992. HMOs spent an average of 9% of their operating expenses per plan on drugs in 1993, as they had in 1992. However, total expenses in 1993 were estimated at $5.3 billion for the industry for outpatient drugs, up from $4.5 billion in 1992.[16]

A survey of 2,395 employers conducted by Foster Higgins reported that in 1993, the cost of prescription drugs rose an average of 15.3% over 1992 costs, almost double the 8% rise of overall benefits costs.[17]

According to the Pharmaceutical Research and Manufacturers of America (PhRMA), it costs $231 million in research costs to bring just one new drug to market.

Why Are Some Drugs So Expensive?

Both as corporate and individual expenses, drug costs have risen in recent years, as have the costs of housing, cars, food and health care in general. It might help to understand why drugs in particular can be relatively costly.

A major component of drug costs is the extensive research and development behind every new drug that goes on the market. The 100 largest drug companies in the United States (part of a $55 billion a year industry) invest nearly $11 billion in research and development annually, according to the PhRMA. It costs $231 million in research costs to bring just one new drug to market, with $0.16 of every sales dollar reinvested in research. Laboratories, equipment and highly trained and specialized experts are also expensive.

In addition to the cost, a lengthy and arduous process is involved in taking a new drug from discovery through approval by the FDA. According to the PhRMA, 5,000 drugs are tested for every one that is approved. It takes an average of 12 years to usher a drug from development to sales including: 3½ years for laboratory and animal studies, six years for human clinical trials and 2½ years for government regulatory review.

Cost-Containment Versus Cost-Effectiveness

> Five thousand drugs are tested for every one approved by the FDA.

It is tempting—and common—to take a shortsighted view of the cost of drug therapy in treating illness. In many cases, a slightly more expensive drug for a particular illness or condition may be the best choice in the long run because it works faster and is more effective than lower priced drugs, and it often can be used at lower dosages. The more expensive drug may need to be taken less often and may also come in a more user-friendly package, which tends to make patients more compliant with the full course of therapy. In addition, there may be fewer side effects associated with the more expensive drug. The product may also come with value-added services such as patient and physician education materials and services. As a result of all these factors, the somewhat higher priced drug is more likely to be effective the first time it's prescribed, cutting down on future doctor visits, additional prescriptions, hospitalization and potential surgery.

Along these more global lines, note the difference between drug cost-containment and cost-effectiveness, two terms that are sometimes used interchangeably but have very different meanings. In the early years of managed care, the focus

> The emphasis of managed care has shifted from cost-containment to cost-effectiveness.

was on *cost-containment*, with such strategies as preferred pricing and discounts. Today's focus, *cost-effectiveness*, takes a broader view of the impact of all relevant aspects of drug therapy as an important part of patient care. Questions like these are now being asked: Is the drug in question not only economical, but also medically effective in both the short term and the long term? What clinical outcomes does the drug produce, and what effect does its use have on other health care expenses? Can it, for example, reduce an employee's length of hospital stay, affect the number and type of lab tests required, influence the number and dosage of other medications, cut the number of doctor office visits and encourage patient compliance with treatment?

The bottom line is this: A drug is truly cost-effective when it offers the same positive results as another form of therapy, such as surgery, *but at a lower cost*.

The cost of pharmaceuticals to employers (also referred to as *payers*) must be considered within the context of total health care spending, not isolated from other medical expenses. Too often, employers and health plan administrators both make the mistake of cutting spending on pharmaceuticals too quickly, without stepping back to look at the big picture. For example, say a company's pharmacy benefit costs have been rising at the rate of 12% annually. Instead of quickly enacting cost cutting measures on drugs alone, the benefits manager should realize that these costs, though they seem high, may be at the best possible level to provide appropriate drug benefits. Though it seems paradoxical, total health care expenses might actually decline if spending for drugs increases to support the optimum use of pharmaceuticals in overall patient care.

A drug is truly cost-effective when it offers the same positive results as another form of therapy but at a lower cost.

What Is Pharmacy Benefits Management?

For cost, quality and accessibility reasons, pharmacy benefits, like all other employee benefits, must now be managed. *Pharmacy benefits management* can be defined as a range of organizational activities designed to influence the behavior of prescribers, pharmacists and patients, with the goal of impacting the cost and use of prescription drug coverage. Drug therapy has become costly, complex and important enough to justify this organizational oversight, management and intervention in the drug use process.

A number of interrelated parties are involved and affected by the process of pharmacy benefits management. They include:

◗ Health plan members (subscribers/enrollees), who become patients when they're ill
◗ Pharmacies that participate in the benefits program as providers of prescription drugs and services
◗ Prescribers (physicians)
◗ Drug manufacturers
◗ Payers, who may be self-funded employers, insurance companies, managed care plans or the government, as with the Medicare and Medicaid programs.

Looking to PBMs for Help

In increasing numbers, payers are choosing to contract with pharmacy benefits management (PBM) firms. What these companies do, and how benefits managers can best interact with them when they choose to, is an important theme of this book. The information in this first chapter is meant to be an introduction and overview of the process of pharmacy benefits management and the companies that offer these services. (See Chapter 8 for a detailed discussion of PBM selection and evaluation.) Subsequent chapters contain more detail on nearly every aspect mentioned here.

> *Payers are increasingly choosing to contract with pharmacy benefits management companies (PBMs).*

Currently proliferating at a rapid rate, PBMs may take the form of a health maintenance organization (HMO), preferred provider organization (PPO), third party administrator (TPA), insurance carrier or specialized PBM. They vary in size, scope and sophistication, but they all operate similarly. PBMs provide external management of a company's pharmacy benefits by applying various managed care principles and procedures in order to contain costs and enhance quality and plan member access to the benefit.

Some of the services PBMs offer, either as an inclusive package, on a menu basis, or as a mix customized for a particular client, include:
◗ Contract price negotiations with drug companies for discounted fees or capitated rates
◗ Rebate contracting
◗ Development and management of a network of preferred pharmacy providers, either chains or independents
◗ Reimbursement of retail pharmacies

○ Drug formulary development and management
○ Claims processing
○ Drug utilization review (DUR), prospective, concurrent and/or retrospective
○ Patient monitoring
○ Generic substitution programs
○ Therapeutic substitution programs
○ Academic detailing programs
○ Outcomes and pharmacoeconomic research
○ Mail-order processing.

Managed Healthcare's 1995 *Directory of Pharmacy Benefits Management Companies* lists 81 PBM companies. They range in size from industry giants covering 56 million lives and handling 350 million prescriptions a year to small, specialized PBMs with 7,000 lives and 80,000 prescriptions per year.

PBMs wield growing influence in the managed prescription drug benefits arena. They are not new, but many people think they are because they have become so much more numerous and visible in the last few years.

The Evolution of Pharmacy Benefits Management

The evolution of pharmacy benefits management until now has focused on four successive areas of concern: (1) enhancing accessibility of pharmacy services and increasing the efficiency of drug benefits administration; (2) containing costs of drug benefits by focusing on price per prescription; (3) obtaining lower costs by focusing on prescription utilization; and (4) managing disease states and patient outcomes. These aren't separate and distinct areas; in fact, the PBM industry is currently fine-tuning its price orientation, refining its utilization strategies and beginning to move into more sophisticated and complex areas like disease state management (discussed at length in Chapter 6).

There have been five stages (so far) in the development of pharmacy benefits management. However, there has been, and continues to be, a lot of overlap in this evolutionary process. For instance, some health plans are still in stage 1 or 2, while others are blazing new trails in stage 5. Generally, though, PBMs have developed along the following lines:

Stage 1: Direct pay
Stage 2: Access-oriented third party administrators (TPAs)
Stage 3: Price-conscious third party administrators (TPAs)
Stage 4: PBMs–influencing the drug use process
Stage 5: PBMs–managing diseases.

Stage 1: Direct Pay

In this first stage, patients pay for their prescriptions at the time they are filled, usually on a fee-for-service basis. Purchasing a prescription is much like buying any other service, except that a physician's authorization is necessary. No restrictions are placed on the prescriber's range of options. Essentially, the prescriber specifies what the member should purchase, but the member has free choice in pharmacies.

If the member has major medical insurance, some of this expense may be paid by the insurer. At the time of service or at year's end, plan members may submit receipts for prescription purchases for reimbursement. If the calendar year deductible has been met, the member is reimbursed for a portion of those expenses.

At one point, direct patient pay (with or without major medical) was the predominant method of paying for prescriptions in community and chain pharmacies. As recently as 1982, nearly three-quarters of prescriptions dispensed were paid directly by the patient.[18] By 1993, just 50% of prescriptions were paid directly, with the remainder paid by public and private drug plans.[19]

Stage 2: Access-Oriented Third Party Administrators (TPAs)

This stage is characterized by the early drug card programs and by many state Medicaid programs, where the purpose is to increase the accessibility of drug therapy by reducing barriers to care. A TPA hired by the payer organizes and maintains the pharmacy network in addition to processing claims. In this stage, members have free choice of pharmacies when the TPA uses an open network (a network in which any pharmacy that agrees to the TPA's conditions can participate).

On behalf of the payer, the TPA issues eligibility cards to members, pays claims to pharmacies and invoices the payer. The TPA may also have a real-time, online point-of-sale (POS) system that links the pharmacy to the PBM by computer.

In addition to receiving a member copayment, the pharmacy submits a claim and receives the remainder of its payment directly from the TPA, according to a fee-for-service reimbursement formula established by the TPA that includes the cost of the product plus a dispensing fee. The TPA is also paid on a fee-for-service basis by the payer based on the number of paid claims.

The early card programs offered three advantages. First, they made access easier by reducing out-of-pocket price. Second, administering drug coverage is not an easy task, and TPAs offered an efficient way of administering coverage for prescription drugs. Drug coverage is marked by numerous claims or transactions, with each involving a small dollar amount. In contrast, hospital insurance has a relatively small number of claims, but each represents a large dollar amount. Consequently, a firm specializing in drug benefits administration can take advantage of economies of scale and develop appropriate systems and networks less expensively than nonspecialists. In other words, rather than develop networks and computer systems for claims processing themselves, insurance companies could buy these services from a TPA. Finally, the third advantage of a card program is that it offers better data to use in monitoring and managing the benefit. This became more important as benefits management continued to evolve and priorities shifted from a focus on access to focuses involving cost control.

Stage 3: Price-Conscious Third Party Administrators (TPAs)

This stage is similar to stage 2, except that the emphasis changed from expanding access to containing costs. For TPA customers (the buyers of pharmacy benefits), the cost advantages associated with a closed network where pharmacy choice is limited took precedence over the patient's ease of access in an open network. In negotiating with pharmacies, TPAs learned that they could trade their volume of business for discounted prices if a limited number of pharmacies were involved. Also, a closed network allows for easier monitoring of pharmacy performance and facilitates the implementation of special programs.

Stage 4: PBMs–Influencing the Drug Use Process

As the cost of pharmacy benefits continued to rise, a natural next step in cost-containment was to address prescribing or utilization patterns. This led to the creation of specialized pharmacy benefits managers (PBMs) with their more interventionist approach to the drug use process and prescribing decisions.

A PBM differs from a TPA in that it attempts to control expenses by intervening in how drugs are prescribed and used. The PBM may perform the same claims processing and price-oriented administrative activities as the TPA in the previous stage, but the PBM is also involved in clinical or drug use decisions and programs to influence prescribing. These include drug use reviews (DURs), formularies, prior authorization, prescribing guidelines and disease management (all described in detail in subsequent chapters).

Stage 5: PBMs–Managing Diseases

At this writing, this fifth stage is in its infancy. *Disease state man-*

agement (DSM) is often referred to as the next generation of managed care because it takes the concept of improving cost, quality and access one step further by targeting chronic, costly medical conditions that require continuing care. Through a combination of pharmaceuticals, practice guidelines, data management, and patient and provider interventions, DSM aims to control the cost of certain diseases by utilizing the most effective treatment modalities as early in a patient's "disease state" as possible. DSM integrates drug therapy with other services and focuses on the costs and outcomes of alternative means of treating a disease. Comprehensive economic data and patient outcomes studies are very important in effective disease management.

PBMs, like managed care, are here to stay. In fact, almost all HMOs and PPOs already contract with PBMs. PBMs, though relatively young, are being forced to change dramatically in order to survive. They must be willing to assume risk, comply with increasingly restrictive formulary requirements and develop value-added programs such as provider and patient education and compliance management. PBMs' future development will be influenced by both the buyers of pharmacy benefits and the suppliers of drugs and services. It remains to be seen how many more stages there will be in the pharmacy benefits management evolution.

> *PBMs, like managed care, are here to stay.*

Endnotes

1. "Health Plans: More Employers Use Carve-Outs," A. Foster Higgins & Co. *Highlights*, May 1995, 1.

2. Marion Merrell Dow, *Managed Care Digest*/HMO Edition, 1994, 33.

3. "PBMs Take Center Stage," *Managed Care Selling Edge*, 1 (2) (September/October 1994): 8.

4. "How Top Company Executives View Drug Benefits," *Business & Health* Special Report, Data Watch 1991, 5.

5. "The Contributions of Pharmaceutical Companies: What's at Stake for America," executive summary. (Boston: The Boston Consulting Group, Inc., September 1993): 3-5.

6. S. Siegelman, "An Expensive Drug May Be the Most Cost-Effective," *Business & Health* Special Report 6 (1991): 9-14.

7. Ibid.

8. "The Contributions of Pharmaceutical Companies," 6.

9. Ibid.

10. *Good Medicine: A Report on the Status of Pharmaceutical Research* (Washington, DC: Pharmaceutical Research and Manufacturers of America, 1992).

11. M. F. Conlan, "Who Does What in Industry Is a Mystery to Many Observers," *Drug Topics* (1992): 66, 72.

12. P. R. Vagelos, "Are Prescription Drug Prices High?" *Science* 252 (1991): 1080-1084.

13. 1993 CENSUS Survey: International Foundation of Employee Benefit Plans.

14. J. Heenan. "Prescription Drug Benefits in a Managed Care Plan: Balancing Quality and Costs," *Medical Interface*, January 1994, 85.

15. R. Navarro, "Pharmacy Management Primer Series: Introduction," *Medical Interface*, September 1992, 42.

16. Marion Merrell Dow, *Managed Care Digest*/HMO Edition, 1994, 5.

17. J. Mandelker, "The Expanding Role of PBMs," *Business & Health* Special Report, 1995, 7.

18. *American Druggist*, May 1995, 17-26.

19. *Drug Topics*, July 25, 1994, 33.

Benefit *plan design* refers to the agreement between you (the employer/payer) or your designated plan administrator/manager and the individual enrollees, also referred to as *members, subscribers* or *patients*. Benefit design basics include such issues as what drugs the plan covers (and doesn't cover), in what quantities, from what pharmacies or other drug sources, and at what out-of-pocket cost to members. Plan design also involves such operational issues as pharmacy reimbursement, claims processing and utilization review.

The importance of the basic plan design itself cannot be overemphasized. It doesn't matter whether you are creating a new pharmacy benefits plan, improving an existing one or preparing to work with a pharmacy benefits management (PBM) company. If your basic plan is not well thought out and tailored to your company's own needs and circumstances, it will make little difference how effective the other components of benefits management are. All the parts of pharmacy benefits management are interrelated, but the long-term quality and effectiveness of your overall plan begins with how well the benefits are designed.

In order to make sure the solution fits the problem, you first need to *do a careful analysis* of your company's benefits budget status and constraints, claims experience, and employee and dependent demographics. This initial step is critical; don't be

Chapter 2...
Pharmacy Benefit Plan Design

> *The importance of the basic plan design itself can't be overemphasized.*

tempted to skip it or hurry through it. Determine what your areas of difficulty or vulnerability are or could be so that benefits can be designed to address or, even better, prevent these problems.

The second step is just as important: *Set some clear, specific goals* that you want your pharmacy benefits to meet. If you don't set goals at the beginning of the process, how will you know if and when you've achieved your objectives? Evaluate prescription drug benefits in the context of your total health care package. As discussed in Chapter 1, well-designed pharmacy benefits can reduce health care costs in general and offset other medical and/or mental health expenses by substituting drug therapy for more expensive treatment such as hospitalization and surgery. Decide how pharmacy benefits could potentially have an optimal impact on your health care expenses, then develop goals based on this "best case" scenario. Given your company's employee and dependent population, what aspects of a drug benefit program are most important to you and to your employees: accessibility, convenience, economy, quality?

> *Set clear, specific, realistic goals for your pharmacy benefits.*

It can be helpful to review the experience of other companies of similar size and demographic composition to see what has or has not worked well for them. Remember, though, that every company is different. Your major concern, for instance, might be the cost of drug benefits, while another business with a larger number of retirees might need to focus more on the convenience and accessibility of obtaining prescription drugs.

Make sure your goals are realistic. Beware of expecting too much with unrealistic goals and setting yourself up for disappointment or failure. It's better to set modest goals (especially with a new program or new relationship with a PBM) and achieve them than to fail to meet objectives that just weren't feasible in the first place.

Be specific. If your primary goal is to reduce costs, for example, don't leave it at that. Set an annual per capita cost target for a certain amount of money saved or a particular percentage in reduced costs.

Characteristics of an Effective Pharmacy Benefit

Your overall goal, of course, is to create pharmacy benefits that meet your employees' needs at a reasonable cost to you. An effective pharmacy benefit promotes the following features:
- Quality
- Accessibility

◑ Efficiency

◑ Member satisfaction.

Quality involves excellence and meeting expectations. It can be defined in terms of its structure, process and the outcomes of care. The *structure* of pharmacy care has to do with the adequacy of the personnel, facilities and technology that provide your pharmacy services. Consider questions like these: Do the professionals providing care have the appropriate training and credentials? Do the pharmacies or other facilities where care is delivered have access to modern equipment and technology?

The *process* of care focuses on the specific services provided to members and how they are performed. Are the procedures and services medically necessary? Does the care being given conform to current and accepted medical knowledge? Do members receive appropriate drugs accompanied by appropriate pharmacy services, such as counseling and monitoring?

Finally, *outcomes* of care refer to what happens to a patient as a result of care; in other words, the effect of the service on the member's health status. Did the patient's health improve as a result of care? How did pharmacy benefit services affect the member's quality of life and productivity at work?

A second characteristic of effective pharmacy benefits is *accessibility*, which refers to minimizing barriers to receiving pharmacy benefits. The pharmacy benefit itself reduces the member's financial barriers to receiving prescription drugs and services. Other barriers might be issues of transportation or geography. The number and location of pharmacies available to your members (or the ease of mail-order pharmacy) are important factors in ensuring that benefits are accessible.

An effective pharmacy benefit promotes quality, accessibility, efficiency and member satisfaction.

A third element of effective pharmacy benefits is *efficiency*. That is, are available resources used wisely? Objectives should be accomplished with the least expensive combination of resources. For example, drug therapy is inefficient if unnecessary drugs are prescribed, or if expensive drugs are prescribed when a less expensive alternative would be equally effective.

The fourth element of effective pharmacy benefits, which is (or should be) related to quality, is *member satisfaction*. This can involve interpersonal as well as technical aspects of care. Do your members feel that their drug benefits are of high quality? Are they accessible? Are they affordable? Are they convenient to access and pay for? Do participating pharmacists treat patients courteously and adequately explain the drugs being dispensed?

The Ideal Pharmacy Benefits Plan

According to the *National Pharmaceutical Council Prescription Medicine Benefit Program Checklist,*[1] benefits managers and the companies they represent want a pharmacy benefit plan that:

- ◑ Covers medications that are effective in treating patients but also reduces overall medical costs
- ◑ Allows prescribers the flexibility to select medications that meet the needs of individual patients
- ◑ Gives plan members the freedom to choose a pharmacy that is readily accessible to them
- ◑ Encourages written instruction sheets, medications monitoring and personalized counseling by the pharmacist
- ◑ Monitors patient compliance with drug therapy
- ◑ Maintains and utilizes patient medication records to prevent unnecessary and potentially harmful drug interactions and other problems (called "medication misadventures"; see Chapter 5 for more on this topic)
- ◑ Employs strict quality assessment standards
- ◑ Conducts appropriate review of drug utilization
- ◑ Promotes prudent patient utilization of benefits by plan members with strategies that may include copayments or plan limitations.

Basic Elements of the Pharmacy Benefit Plan

Basic plan elements include:

1. *Member cost-sharing*
2. *Pharmacy reimbursement*
3. *Plan limitations, restrictions and exclusions*
4. *Provider network*
5. *Claims processing and administration*
6. *Data collection*
7. *Drug utilization review (DUR)*
8. *Communication.*

There are certain basic elements of an effective pharmacy benefit plan that will be defined or briefly explained in this chapter. A number of these elements, however, are sufficiently important that they will be discussed in far more detail later in this guidebook. Several even have whole chapters devoted to them.

Member Cost-Sharing

Member cost-sharing refers to the part of the cost of drugs that members are required to pay out of pocket. There are three major types of cost-sharing: (a) *copayments*, (b) *coinsurance* and (c) *deductibles*.

A *copayment* (also referred to as a *copay*) is a set dollar amount for each unit of service; for example, a member pays $10 per prescription no matter what its actual cost. *Coinsurance* is a percentage of the cost of each drug dispensed (for instance, 20%) that the member pays. A *deductible* is a dollar amount that must be paid out of pocket before a member's insurance coverage begins.

There are advantages to each of these three types of cost-sharing. The advantage of a copayment is that it's an amount known in advance by both the member and the plan manager, and that makes it easy to predict and administer. The advantage of coinsurance is that (theoretically at least) it promotes cost-consciousness. Members have the incentive to buy a less expensive product so that their out-of-pocket expense will be less. Finally, a calendar year deductible has the advantage to plan administrators of being a source of protection against large, unanticipated or catastrophic expenses.

Copayments are the most common form of cost-sharing. In the early days of prescription card programs when claims were submitted by mail after the purchase was complete, it was the only feasible form of cost-sharing. Since the plan administrator determined the allowable price of a prescription, an accurate coinsurance amount was difficult or impossible to calculate at the time of purchase. The same problem held true for the deductible, which the pharmacist also had no way of knowing. Today, with what's called *online adjudication* through *point-of-sale systems*, the plan administrator and the pharmacy communicate via computer as prescriptions are being filled, making the use of both coinsurance and deductibles possible.

Member copayments (usually between $4 and $8 per prescription) are collected when the prescription is filled, and this amount is deducted from what the plan administrator pays to the pharmacy. For instance, if a prescription has an allowable price of $20 and the copayment is $5, the pharmacy would receive $5 from the member and the remaining $15 from the plan administrator.

Cost-sharing affects the total cost of prescription drug benefits in two ways: It affects the amount paid for each prescription, and it also affects utilization. According to the law of demand in economics, as price increases, demand tends to decrease. In the case of drug prescriptions, price is the member's out-of-pocket expense. As cost-sharing (i.e., out-of-pocket expense) increases, utilization decreases.

The most comprehensive study done on patient cost-sharing, the RAND Health Insurance Experiment, found that as the out-of-pocket expense went from 0% to 25%, the quantity of prescriptions purchased decreased 18% and total expenditures for prescription drugs decreased 23%.[2] This study applied cost-sharing to all health care services, including physician visits, where the demand for drugs begins. (According to the National Center for Health Statistics, three of every five doctor office visits result in a prescription.) If cost-sharing reduces visits to physicians and other prescribers, prescriptions are also likely to be reduced. The authors concluded that the change in prescription drug expenditures was due to decreased exposure to physicians and the resulting lower number of prescriptions, rather than a search for lower prescription prices. Changes in cost-sharing that apply only to prescriptions may have a different effect on the demand for drugs.

> *Cost-sharing can be designed to reward desirable behaviors.*

Cost-sharing can be set up to reward desired behaviors. This is the case with incentives to use *generic products*, which are usually less expensive than brand-name drugs. Generic products are chemically equivalent to the brand-name (also called the *originator* or *innovator*) product, which is protected under patent for its first (approximately) seven years on the market. Generics, which are regulated by the FDA, have the same active ingredients in the same strength and in the same dosage form as the originator drug. They are required to show what is called *bioequivalence* with the brand-name product; that is, the generic must enter the blood stream in the same amount of time and quantity as the brand-name product. The FDA publishes the bioequivalence ratings of all products in what is commonly called the *Orange Book*. Most (but not all) generics are thought to be just as safe and effective as their branded counterparts. (Generic products are also discussed in Chapter 4 on formularies.)

In terms of using generics in cost-sharing, three alternatives are available: (1) differential copayments, (2) coinsurance (also called a coinsurance rider) and (3) limiting benefit coverage to the generic price. With differential copayments, a higher copayment applies if a branded product is dispensed when a less expensive generic product is available. For example, a $5 copay may apply to all prescriptions filled with generic products, and a $10 copay to branded products, when available.

As described earlier, coinsurance (cost-sharing as a percentage of the total drug charge) can encourage patients to be more cost-conscious in choosing pharmaceutical products. As the price difference between the brand-name and generic products becomes greater, the incentive of co-insurance to use generics increases. For instance, let's assume that a prescription can be filled with a $60 branded product or a $10 generic product. With 20% coinsurance, the patient must choose between paying $2 out of pocket for the generic versus $12 for the brand-name drug. Naturally, this creates an incentive for patients to choose less expensive drugs.

Third, benefits can be limited to the price of the generic product. If a plan member requests a brand-name drug, he or she is responsible for paying the difference between the brand price and the generic price. If, for example, a plan has a copay of $5 for every prescription, and benefits are limited to the price of the generic, the member with a choice of a $60 brand product or $10 generic version faces these options: $5 for the generic product or $55 for the brand-name one (the $50 price difference plus the $5 copay).

In every state, drug product selection laws and regulations specify means by which the prescriber can mandate the use of a branded product. When the *prescriber* insists upon a brand-name drug, then is the patient responsible for paying the price difference between the brand-name and the generic drugs? The answer depends on the benefit design. On one hand, the design can hold the patient harmless for prescriber decisions and not require that the difference be paid. On the other hand, in plans where the goal is to encourage the use of generic products, patients may be required to pay the price difference, even though the decision to go with the brand-name drug was not theirs. This gives patients plenty of incentive to request that their doctor prescribe generics whenever possible.

According to the Marion Merrell Dow, *Managed Care Digest*/HMO Edition, 1994,[3] in 1993 the average copayment (except for Medicare and Medicaid) for brand-name drugs was $6.78 per prescription, or 31% of prescription costs. The average copay for generic drugs was $4.75 per prescription, or 31% of prescription costs. Copayments were required on non-formulary drugs by 71% of HMOs, on formulary drugs by 79% of plans and on both generic and brand-name drugs by 98% of HMOs. Less than 1% required no copayments for prescription drugs.

Pharmacy Reimbursement

Pharmacy reimbursement consists of a variety of factors, but the basic components are:

◐ A dispensing fee (a set amount paid to a pharmacist by the plan ad-

ministrator per prescription order filled) that is added to the ingredient cost of the medication
- ◗ Ingredient cost of the drug, which can be based on an average wholesale price (AWP), maximum allowable cost (MAC), estimated acquisition cost (EAC) or actual acquisition cost (AAC). (Note: These terms are all covered in Chapter 4 and defined in the glossary.)

Plan Limitations, Restrictions and Exclusions

Plan limitations, restrictions and exclusions are major cost-containment elements of pharmacy benefits plan design. There are numerous types of limitations that are used to widely varying degrees in different plans. One is a cap, or limit, on outpatient drug benefits, usually $2,000 a year per member. Another is the *formulary* (a restricted list of reimbursable medications), discussed in detail in Chapter 4.

Another very common limitation involves the *quantity* of drugs dispensed at one time. In other words, the plan will pay for only a limited supply of medication at once. A typical arrangement is that the plan pays for either a 30-day supply or 100 units of a prescribed drug. A variation on this is a plan that pays for a two-week initial supply, followed by a 30- to 90-day supply for refills. (Refills, by the way, are usually subject to state regulations, which may limit refills to a one-year period from the original date of prescription.)

Coverage exclusions (which drugs are covered and which aren't) can play a big part in plan limitations strategy.

One alternative to the above limitation is to allow large quantities (say, a three- to six-month supply) to be prescribed at once for chronic conditions, as with asthma. The opposite of this approach is to limit all prescriptions to a 30-day supply. The advantages of a larger supply are increased convenience for the patient and a reduced number of dispensing fees for pharmacists. The advantages of a smaller supply are less wasted product if a prescription is discontinued, more cost-sharing when a co-payment is used and closer monitoring of the patient's drug use.

The category of *coverage limitations* (that is, which drugs are covered and which are not) often plays a big part in plan limitations. Typically, drugs that are only available by prescription (also called *legend drugs*) are covered when authorized by a professional for the treatment of a medical condition. That is, the prescriber is saying the drug is medically necessary.

Typically, over-the-counter (OTC) or nonprescription drugs are not covered by insurance. (Insulin for diabetes is usually exempt from this rule.)

The rationale is that most OTC products are affordable to patients without insurance. Insurance coverage of OTC products could easily be abused by plan members and become expensive to the payer. In addition to these issues, not all nonprescription products have undergone FDA review for safety and effectiveness, so their medical necessity may be in question.

The prescription versus OTC issue is becoming more complex because an increasing number of drugs are being switched from prescription-only status to over the counter. Should these OTC products be covered if they're prescribed by authorized providers? Some experts feel that coverage of selected prescribed OTC products should be allowed because it may enhance the overall efficacy of drug therapy and consequently improve the pharmacy benefit. According to the Marion Merrell Dow, *Managed Care Digest*/HMO Edition, 1994, 13% of all HMOs cover some OTC medications.[4]

A second category of drugs that many plans do not cover is referred to as *drug efficacy study implementation (DESI) drugs*. These are drugs that were reclassified by the FDA in 1962 as safe, but they have not been proven fully effective under today's regulations. Coverage is occasionally extended to certain categories of DESI drugs that have been tested to some extent for efficacy.

Third, *experimental drugs* are usually excluded from coverage, just as health insurance policies don't cover experimental therapies or procedures. Deciding whether or not a drug is experimental is easier than deciding whether a type of surgery, for instance, is experimental because the safety and efficacy of a drug must be demonstrated in large clinical trials before the FDA allows it on the market. Once a drug earns FDA approval, it's no longer considered experimental. Experimental drugs were excluded from prescription coverage by 95% of all HMOs in 1993.[5]

Other prescription drugs commonly excluded from coverage included most injectables (except insulin), anorexiants (appetite suppressants), smoking cessation products, fertility drugs and oral contraceptives. Vitamins were excluded by 40% of HMOs. Prescriptions for cosmetic purposes were covered by just 6% of HMOs. Other drugs sometimes excluded are hormones, allergens, immunosuppressives/AZT, behavioral modification drugs, biological serums, cough syrup, dental, fluorides, inhalants, Retin-A, and medical devices and apparatus.[6]

A related issue is the use of drugs for unapproved or *off-label* indications. The FDA approves drugs for very specific indications or uses for which the drug has been proven to be safe and effective. Once a drug is on the market, though, it's often used for additional purposes. However, when these new indications have not been subject to the rigorous scientific study involved in FDA approval, the question is: Do off-label uses constitute experimental use? This has been a heavily debated issue in recent years. The current trend is to cover approved drugs even when they are used for an off-label indication. However, as very expensive drugs such as the new biotechnology products come on the market and are used for off-label indications, the issue is likely to remain complex and controversial.

A very different type of plan limitation involves a *prior authorization program*, where the drug has to be approved by the plan administrator or benefits manager on a case-by-case basis before it's covered. Generally, a prior authorization program applies to specific drugs that are expensive, risky or whose effectiveness is limited to certain situations. Prior authorizations can be inconvenient at the very least because of the time the approval process may take and the delay in getting a needed prescription filled.

Provider Network

Provider network refers to the network of pharmacies with which the health plan has contracted and from which members must choose when they have prescriptions filled. This topic is covered in detail in Chapter 3.

Claims Processing and Administration

Claims processing and administration is a very basic element of a pharmacy benefits program. There are three methods involved:
1. *Direct claim:* The plan member pays for the prescription at the pharmacy, then submits a claims form for reimbursement.
2. *Card system:* Plan members are issued cards to be presented at the pharmacy when a prescription is filled. Plan and patient information may be embossed or contained on a magnetic strip on the card. This data is relayed by the pharmacy to the claims payer to collect payment.
3. *Point of service (POS):* An electronic system for exchanging information (such as eligibility, plan limits, copayment amounts, product information, etc.) between the pharmacy and the claims administrator at the time the pharmacist dispenses the prescription.

Data Collection

Data collection involves gathering the data required for drug utilization review (DUR), outcomes research and other purposes.

Drug Utilization Review (DUR)

Drug utilization review (DUR), which is discussed in detail in Chapter 5, has four major components:

1. Measuring or monitoring physician prescribing behavior, pharmacist dispensing patterns and patient drug use
2. Management, or determining the cause of over- or underprescribing of certain drugs
3. Feedback to the provider and, sometimes, intervention in the form of education
4. Reassessment by the plan following intervention to determine if it was successful in changing behavior.

Communication

Communication is essential among benefits managers, plan members, plan administrators, pharmacies and prescribers about all the issues that affect them individually and as a group. An effective managed pharmacy benefit requires that everyone involved work together. (Communication is discussed in Chapter 8.)

Questions to Ask About Plan Design

1. Does your firm offer benefit plan design consulting services? What does this involve, and what are the average costs?

2. By what method do you determine the feasibility of a pharmacy benefit plan for individual clients?

3. Do you survey employee demographics and, if so, how?

4. What type of cost-sharing does your plan design utilize? Is it sufficient to generate cost-consciousness among members?

5. What, if any, are your incentives to use generic products (differential copayments, coinsurance, paying difference in price if brand name is requested or prescribed, etc.)?

6. How is the decision to substitute generic products made?

7. What restrictions in coverage, if any, apply to:
   ◑ Quantity of drugs allowed per prescription
   ◑ DESI drugs
   ◑ Experimental drugs
   ◑ Off-label drugs
   ◑ Drugs used for cosmetic purposes
   ◑ Other classes of drugs.

8. Do you have a prior authorization program in place? Describe it. Which products are included?

HOW PRESCRIPTIONS DRUGS ARE COVERED IN RELATION TO OVERALL HEALTH PLANS[7]

	Indemnity	PPO	POS	HMO
Number of employees	633	481	225	684
Comprehensive plan				
With no generic or mail-order incentive	52%	31%	15%	5%
With generic incentive	7%	7%	3%	1%
With mail-order incentive	7%	7%	4%	<1%
With combinations of mail-order and generic incentives	12%	12%	10%	1%
Drug card plan (100% after copay)				
With no generic or mail-order incentive	5%	11%	24%	63%
With generic incentive	9%	17%	26%	25%
With mail-order incentive	1%	2%	2%	<1%
With combination of mail-order and generic incentives	6%	13%	16%	3%
Other (e.g., greater of % of cost or copay)	1%	<1%	—	1%
	100%	100%	100%	100%

9. Who are the participating pharmacies in your network(s)? What are the criteria for participation?

10. What method of claims processing and administration do you use (direct claim, card, POS, etc.)?

11. What does your DUR program involve?

12. By what methods do you encourage communication among plan members, payers and others?

Endnotes

1. National Pharmaceutical Council Prescription Medicine Benefit Program Checklist (Reston, VA: National Pharmaceutical Council, 1990).

2. A. Leibowitz, W. G. Manning and J. P. Newhouse, "The Demand for Prescription Drugs as a Function of Cost Sharing," *Social Science and Medicine* 21 (1985): 1063-1069.

3. Marion Merrell Dow, *Managed Care Digest*/HMO Edition, 1994, 33.

4. Ibid.

5. Ibid., 34.

6. Ibid.

7. "Preretirement Medical," *Salaried Employee Benefits Provided by Major U.S. Employers in 1994* (Lincolnshire, IL: Hewitt Associates, 1994), 36.

his chapter will discuss the organizational and financial relationships between a pharmacy benefits manager and those pharmacies that participate in the plan's network. (Note: The terms *pharmacy benefits manager* and *PBM* are used in this and subsequent chapters to refer to whoever is managing the pharmacy benefits—whether that's you from within the company or a specialized firm with whom you've contracted. As Chapter 8 discusses in detail, many employers today are choosing to hire pharmacy benefits management *companies*, so the term will most often refer to these external managers.)

The chapter is divided into five sections. The first defines and describes the different options for the *delivery* of outpatient pharmacy services. The second section describes the methods of *reimbursing pharmacies* for the services they provide and the incentives associated with each. It also looks at the evaluation of the various methods. (This is an area that's changing fast and becoming more complex all the time. The intent here is to provide an overview of current practices and trends and take a look into the immediate future.) The third section explores *claims processing and point-of-sale technology*. The fourth section looks at how a pharmacy benefits manager can define and monitor the *quality* of network pharmacies. Finally, the fifth section reviews *member satisfaction* with pharmacy services.

Chapter 3...

Pharmacy Network Development

Delivery Options for Outpatient Pharmacy Services

Delivering drugs from the hands of the manufacturer to those of the consumer has become a lot more complicated than it used to be. Until the 1980s, there was only one place to have a doctor's prescription filled: the local drugstore. Back then, when health care in general was a lot simpler, drugs moved in a fairly straight line from the manufacturer, to the wholesaler, to the pharmacy and then to the consumer. Today, there are a number of drug distribution channels health plans may use, and that in itself makes pharmacy plan design challenging.

This variety of distribution mechanisms (including choices such as preferred pharmacy providers, mail-order services, company-owned pharmacies and HMO pharmacies) was developed in an effort to contain rising drug costs. In the fee-for-service days when drug benefits were nearly always part of major medical health insurance, plan members' costs were typically reimbursed no matter where prescriptions were filled. But today, because of rising expense, managed care has encouraged the creation of a number of distribution avenues to control costs and increase efficiency.

Today, managed care organizations (MCOs) can contract with a retail pharmacy chain, an independent, or what is called a *pharmacy service administration organization (PSAO)*. A PSAO is an organized network of independent pharmacies created to market and administer competitive prescription drug programs to HMOs and PPOs. A PSAO gives its members volume buying power and can also administer claims processing and reimbursement in order to compete with pharmacy chains in the marketplace.

Five Major Types of Delivery Options

There are currently five major types of delivery options being used by managed pharmacy benefit plans. Each can be used separately or in combination with one or two others.

1. An *open network* is a network of pharmacies in which any

pharmacy may participate if it is willing to accept the terms of the insurance plan's contract. (Some states have "any willing provider" statutes that mandate the inclusion of any provider willing to comply with the contract's terms.) The major advantage of the open network is convenient access for plan members. If many pharmacies participate, plan members have an almost unrestricted choice of pharmacies. They can select the pharmacy they like best or the one that's most convenient, and they can also switch pharmacies if they want or need to.

2. A *closed network*, on the other hand, is one in which only certain pharmacies, or "preferred providers," may participate. Pharmacy networks are formed when PBMs, HMOs, PPOs or TPAs (third party administrators) contract with a select group of pharmacies to supply prescriptions to plan members at a discounted rate. The pharmacies, in turn, are virtually guaranteed a higher sales volume, since plan members have a strong financial incentive to use network providers.

In order to achieve the goal of cost-containment, a closed network must be large enough to adequately serve plan members, but small enough to allow benefits managers to control costs through the policies and parameters set for providers. This often proves to be a delicate balance.

A closed network has more advantages for benefits managers and pharmacies than it does for plan members because it restricts members' access to certain pharmacies. The arrangement makes it easier for PBMs to set standards and monitor the pharmacies' performance. When any licensed pharmacy can participate, as in an open network, the benefits managers find it more difficult (if not impossible) to monitor the performance or change the behavior of participating providers.

Also, with a closed network of manageable size, the PBM can more easily implement programs designed to control costs or improve patient care, especially when those programs require pharmacy cooperation.

3. *HMO (staff model) pharmacies*, also called *in-house pharmacies*, are owned and operated by the health plan itself and are usually located right in the plan's clinic or health care center. In addition, HMOs may contract with outside pharmacies, utilize a mail-order service (if they don't operate their own) or use a combination of distribution channels.

In-house pharmacies allow HMOs maximum control over cost, quality and customer service because the pharmacy occupies the same physical space as everyone else under the HMO management's control. It's also much easier for pharmacists to consult with the HMO's medical staff, and patients like the convenience of being able to have prescriptions filled where they have just seen the doctor.

In 1993, 24% of staff model HMOs and 22% of group model HMOs used in-house pharmacies exclusively to fill prescriptions.[1] HMOs with their own pharmacies reported that 72% of all prescriptions were filled in-house. Not-for-profit HMOs (36%) were almost twice as likely as other plans to have in-house pharmacies.[2]

4. A fourth delivery channel is reflected by the fact that a number of companies now have their own pharmacies right at the workplace site(s). These are also sometimes called in-house pharmacies but, to avoid confusion in this discussion, we'll call them *company pharmacies*. The exact number of companies that own and operate their own pharmacies is hard to estimate, but their ranks are growing, and it can be an appealing option for certain large employers.

Company pharmacies can negotiate wholesale or near wholesale prices because of the large number of employees they serve. In fact, companies able to fill, say, 200,000 prescriptions a year have bargaining power with manufacturers similar to that of a small pharmacy chain. Some plans are fully subsidized by the company with no copayment or coinsurance required of employees, while others require a small copay. In some plans, beneficiaries can use outside pharmacies if they choose to, but they usually must pay for their prescriptions upfront, then submit claims for reimbursement.

Advantages to employees of company pharmacies include a high degree of convenience and little or no expense. But there can be disadvantages for employers. One large firm, for instance, experienced a noticeable drop in productivity when it put in its own pharmacy because so many employees were taking time off from work to have their prescriptions filled.

Companies considering putting in their own pharmacy should consider the decision carefully. First, a company must be large enough to warrant the expense. A general guideline is that there should be at least 4,000 to 6,000 employees at each site where a pharmacy is being considered, with a volume of at least 150 prescriptions per day. Space is another issue. A company pharmacy requires at least 500 square feet.[3] However, even in the absence of these criteria, high local retail costs or a high volume of employee prescriptions may make a company pharmacy worth considering.

5. A *mail-order* option is another delivery alternative and an especially fast-growing one. Companies that mail certain drugs to plan members can purchase in larger volumes and at better prices, so they can offer discounted prices on prescriptions to employees. Mail order is especially appropriate for long-term drug therapy (as for chronic conditions that require maintenance medication) or with large numbers of retirees, who may find it difficult to visit community pharmacies to have prescriptions filled.

According to the Marion Merrell Dow, *Managed Care Digest*/HMO Edition, 1994, use of mail-order pharmacy services jumped to 23% of all HMOs in 1993, from 16% in 1992. Use of mail order doubled between 1992 and 1993 at staff model HMOs and nearly tripled at group model HMOs. The largest HMOs nationally were most likely to use mail-order services. HMOs with at least 100,000 members were twice as likely as those with fewer than 100,000 members to use mail order in 1993. HMOs less than five years old were more likely than other plans to offer a mail-order option.[4]

Results of a 1993 Prescription Price Watch survey ranked the features that respondents thought were most important in mail-order vendors: At the top of the list was customer service (41%), followed by quality control (21%), managing benefit cost (15%), speed (13%), flexibility (8%) and other (2%). Payers felt that effectively managing cost was more important than vendors did, noting that adequate facilities and timely, accurate dispensing were minimal expectations.

Experts offer the following advice on implementing mail order and choosing a vendor:[5]

- Set a target discount range based on your buying power and accurate discount information.
- Don't assume that mail-order prices are automatically lower than retail. Do some research to make sure this is so in your area.
- Be clear on the tradeoffs between financial incentives and mail-order savings. Some plans are designed in a way that gives all the savings to plan members.
- Do a due diligence search on any vendor you're considering. Ask for written information and references and conduct a site visit.
- Include in the contract provisions for periodic audits to check for duplicate claims, dispense-as-written validity, generic substitution and accurate pricing formulas.

(See Appendix 1 at the end of this chapter for a categorized list of mail service purchasing criteria.)

Some experts feel the cost savings from mail-order plans are debatable. On one hand, mail-order drugs are less expensive on a per unit basis, partly because mail-order pharmacies can buy drugs at reduced prices, and partly because large quantities of drugs are dispensed, which reduces the number of dispensing fees. On the other hand, larger quantities can lead to waste if a prescription is discontinued and lower per unit fees can be offset by high quantities. Some industry observers also worry that patient care may be compromised when plan members get their prescriptions through the mail because there is no personal contact with a pharmacist such as counseling, written information and compliance monitoring, but hard evidence of this shortcoming is lacking so far.

As noted earlier, health plans often use several delivery options in combination to give beneficiaries adequate pharmacy coverage when and where it's needed. For instance, an HMO pharmacy might be combined with a mail-order service for maintenance drug therapy and a contract with one pharmacy chain in the community.

The combined management and coordination of mail and retail delivery options is called *integrated delivery systems (IDS)*.

IDS advantages include:[6]

❍ A single, comprehensive database that simplifies eligibility verification

❍ Increased convenience for plan members

❍ Improved clinical and utilization management in providing a single locus of control

❍ Elimination of duplication in dispensing and administrative functions.

One PBM executive warns that an IDS is simply a technical system that can facilitate but not ensure optimal results. Even the best IDS can't compensate for poor benefit design, inadequate or inaccurate evaluation of financial savings from mail versus retail, or substandard vendors.[7]

(See Appendix 2 for a list of IDS evaluation factors.)

Pharmacy Reimbursement Methods

Network pharmacies can be reimbursed by the pharmacy benefits manager in a number of ways. The list of possibilities is growing as managed pharmacy evolves. This section will discuss six reimbursement methods: (1) product cost plus fee, (2) capitation, (3) risk-sharing, (4) usual and customary (U&C) charges, (5) incentive payments and (6) payments for cognitive services.

Pharmacy Reimbursement Methods

1. *Product cost plus fee*
2. *Capitation*
3. *Risk-sharing*
4. *Usual and customary (U&C) charges*
5. *Incentive payments*
6. *Payments for cognitive services*

Product Cost Plus Fee

A formula called *product cost plus fee*, a fee-for-service arrangement, has, to date, been the most common method of paying pharmacies. The first part of the formula, reimbursement for product cost, is commonly based on the drug's average wholesale price (AWP). This is the list, or book, price of the drug paid by pharmacies (at least theoretically) for the products they buy. In reality, the AWP is often higher–sometimes much higher–than the price the pharmacy actually pays because of various discounts. Therefore, many contracts between PBMs and pharmacies discount the average wholesale price in an effort to compensate pharmacies for what is called the estimated acquisition cost (EAC). For instance, a contract between the PBM and pharmacy may specify reimbursement as "AWP less ___%." The discounts can differ for single source (i.e., brand-name) products versus multisource (generic) products. An example in a recent publication of the American Pharmaceutical Association (APA) is "AWP less 45%" for generic products and "AWP less 10%" for branded products.[8] Another category of cost is the actual acquisition cost (AAC), which refers to the price paid by a pharmacy for a specific quantity of a drug.

Maximum Allowable Cost (MAC)

Some contracts include a *maximum allowable cost (MAC)* provision, which spells out upper limits that a plan will pay for generic and multisource brand drugs. MACs can also apply to brand names with generic competition. As noted above, retail pharmacies and mail-order vendors usually set reimbursement in relation to the AWP (such as "AWP minus 10%"). However, AWPs for generic drugs are artificially high by as much as 40% to 80% compared to the price the pharmacy actually pays (the *AAC*). A MAC can reconcile the difference between an inflated AWP and the AAC, reducing cost to the health plan while still allowing the pharmacy a profit margin.

MACs are derived from a number of places, including major payers, proprietary sources and the Health Care Financing Administration (HCFA). These sources examine databases and look at direct, wholesale and net costs to arrive at MAC prices. Generally, the MAC is established by taking the prices of widely available generic distributors and using the average of these or, alternatively, the lowest of these. Whenever the product is dispensed, the MAC is used in calculating reimbursement, regardless of which manufacturer's version was dispensed. If the pharmacy dispenses a version that is more expensive than the MAC, reimbursement is limited to the MAC amount and the pharmacy loses money.

A national survey showed that only 47% of large employers that responded and 31% of small employers had a MAC in place.[9] A MAC is well worth considering, though. A few tips: In evaluating a vendor's MAC list, ask how many items are included, how it was developed including the size and source of the database, and how often it's updated. Ask your vendor for a periodic report quantifying the dollar amount of your MAC savings.

The second element in the product cost plus fee formula, the *dispensing fee*, is usually fixed; that is, every pharmacy under a particular contract receives the same fee for each prescription dispensed. The use of variable fees (i.e., different fees for different pharmacies) is not widespread at this time. With a single dispensing fee paid to all pharmacies, however, pharmacies with a high-service volume can be penalized.

The dispensing fee can be altered to promote desirable behaviors. For instance, a higher fee might be paid for prescriptions filled with generic products or when other designated services are provided with a prescription. In this case, the fee can vary with the prescription or the value-added service, but the same fee schedule applies to all pharmacies.

There are three advantages to the product cost plus fee method of reimbursing pharmacies: (1) It's easy to administer, (2) it allows the PBM to keep up with pharmacy product price changes and (3) it allows plan members the freedom to change pharmacies. However, as with all fee-for-service pricing, the pharmacist's financial incentives potentially conflict with the interests of the payer. In other words, the pharmacy makes out better financially with higher utilization, while the payer's goal is just the opposite–to limit prescriptions to those that are medically necessary.

To illustrate how this method of reimbursement plays out: In 1992, the Emron Managed Care Prescription Drug Therapeutic Class Audit reported that the average pharmacy reimbursement paid by plans with managed benefits was 10% less than the AWP, with a $2.15 dispensing fee.[10]

Capitation

Capitation, the second reimbursement alternative, has become quite popular, or at least is now being considered by many payers. Capitation is a fixed dollar amount, a negotiated per capita rate prepaid by the health plan to providers. It's usually expressed as *per member per month* or *PMPM*. Capitation is a form of risk-sharing between the pharmacy benefits manager (acting on behalf of the health plan) and the pharmacy provider.

There are three potential capitation relationships:

1. The pharmacy with a capitated contract is paid by the PBM an agreed-upon payment per person, per time period. In a capitated arrangement, a pharmacy receives a monthly fee upfront for each of its plan members, regardless of how many or how few prescriptions they fill that month. If the plan member receives few,

or no, drugs, the pharmacy profits, but if the member has a lot of prescriptions filled, or has prescriptions for expensive drugs in a given month, the pharmacy loses money. The pharmacy, therefore, has a financial incentive to keep costs down whenever possible by using generic or less expensive drugs.

2. HMOs and PBMs sometimes purchase pharmaceuticals together from manufacturers on a capitated basis. In theory, at least, the manufacturer provides an unlimited supply of a specific product for a capitated fee. The plan's costs are fixed. Another version of this concept is for a manufacturer to capitate all drug treatment for a specific disease, perhaps including more than one drug commonly used to treat the disease, along with educational programs to improve compliance.

3. HMOs or PBMs can provide pharmacy benefits to plan sponsors (private or public purchasers of pharmacy benefits) on a capitated basis, yet still reimburse network pharmacies on a discounted fee-for-service basis.[11]

There are three major drawbacks to capitated payments paid to individual pharmacies. First, capitation by definition assumes an average utilization per patient. Over a large number of patients, this average is usually quite accurate. However, within a smaller group of patients, utilization may be much greater (or much less) than the overall average due to *outliers*, those plan subscribers whose drug utilization falls well outside the average range. Consequently, although capitation rates are usually based on past utilization, luck may play a part in the financial outcome of a capitated contract in terms of whether the pharmacy happens to serve predominantly sick or healthy prescription customers.

Second, pharmacies don't directly control the prescribing of the drugs they dispense, which is clearly a major factor in drug utilization. They can't control which drugs will be prescribed, how many drugs will be prescribed or how often prescriptions will be refilled. Therefore, under a capitated system, an individual pharmacy can't really influence utilization much and, consequently, can't influence the cost of the services for which it agrees to assume financial responsibility. A third disadvantage is that patients must select one pharmacy (or a pharmacy from a very short list), so members' freedom of choice is greatly reduced.

Overall, it is much more difficult to capitate individual pharmacies than it is to capitate a pharmacy chain or, for instance, a high-volume mail-order service. Even then, the risks are evident.

Many employers became interested in capitation quite suddenly following the landmark ruling by the Financial Accounting Standards Board

(FASB), FAS #106, which required all employers, beginning in 1993, to record their future obligation to provide medical benefits to retirees as a liability on their financial statements. This was a significant blow to companies with many retirees, especially many over age 65, because a high percentage of older Americans' health care expenses involve medication, and Medicare doesn't pay for outpatient prescription drugs. Capitation seemed to many of these employers to be a quick way to predict expenses and control costs.

Many of the companies that jumped on the capitation bandwagon for this reason were shocked to find that their pharmacy costs continued to be quite high or even went up. Industry analysts attributed one of the reasons this happened to the *shoe box effect*. Under the old indemnity plans, employees often collected their prescription receipts in a shoe box with the intention of filing claims eventually. However, many health plan members never got around to doing that, so plans made money and expenses seemed lower than they would have been if all claims had actually been submitted. With capitation and other managed care strategies like card programs where pharmacies file computerized claims automatically when prescriptions are filled, employers found that in many cases their costs went up, not down. Disenchanted with capitation as a cure for high costs, employers encouraged PBMs to come up with other ways to control pharmacy expenses.

Risk-Sharing

Though capitation is still used, currently a number of more creative (and complicated) types of *risk-sharing* are appearing on the managed pharmacy scene. The newer hybrids vary from one contract to another, but many set an annual cost-per-member target for ingredient cost, that is, the cost of the drugs themselves. If the cost per member turns out to be lower than the target amount, the PBM and employer usually share the savings. If costs exceed the target, the employer pays only half of the extra cost, and the PBM is responsible for the rest. With capitation, in contrast, the employer must spend the full capitated amount per member, whether that cost is actually incurred or not.

According to a leading PBM,[12] many employers are beginning to believe they have more to gain from creative risk-sharing than from a more conservative risk-sharing arrangement like capitation. Risk-sharing pays off for employers that can find ways (usually financial incentives) to influence plan members to use the least expensive drugs available. One advantage of coinsurance is that it helps employees realize the actual cost of drugs because they're required to pay a percentage. The higher the drug cost, the higher their own cost is. With a copayment, the true cost of the drug is hidden (most consumers never know what it is) and members don't pay a penalty for using more expensive drugs.

Even though risk-sharing does allow large employers to budget more accurately, there are two drawbacks. One is that this kind of control by employers usually must restrict employee choices, but the bigger problem is the lack of historical data to show that risk-sharing really works as advertised. At least two years of isolated drug cost data are necessary to accurately fix a target amount, and few companies have that kind of data yet because these arrangements are so recent.

Several benefits consultants note that an increasing number of plan sponsors are asking for capitated and risk-sharing rates in addition to fee-for-service rates in their requests for proposals (RFPs) from PBM companies. (Chapter 8 discusses the PBM selection process in detail.) This trend illustrates that the awareness and interest are there, but a fairly small percentage of companies so far are actually opting for risk-sharing.[13] Most employers seem to prefer to approach heavy management of pharmacy benefits more slowly by implementing such strategies as closed networks or mail-order service first before embarking on a more challenging–and potentially risky–program like creative risk-sharing.

Usual and Customary (U&C) Charges

Another pharmacy reimbursement method, *usual and customary (U&C) charges*, has been commonly used in physician reimbursement for some time and is now being discussed for pharmacy. It involves a complicated formula but, very basically, the "usual" charge is what the individual pharmacy typically charges for a particular prescription, and the "customary" charge is the prevailing charge in that geographic area for the same product.

Paying pharmacies on the basis of U&C is not very common because the method suffers from two major problems. First, U&C only makes economic sense in a price-competitive market because price competition tends to regulate pricing. Without competition, a pharmacy can charge whatever it wants, and a reimbursement plan based on U&C is like writing a blank check. As third party insurance for prescription drugs becomes more widespread, price competition is decreasing because plan members' copayments are the same no matter which pharmacy is used. U&C pricing is also often based on charges to cash paying customers, not prices quoted to PBMs. Cash prices are likely to be higher, so U&C prices don't always reflect the pharmacy's actual pricing structure.

The second reason U&C is not widespread is that prices pharmacies pay for drug products may increase frequently and significantly. Keeping the U&C profile current with price changes is a real challenge.

Incentive Payments

A very recent development in pharmacy reimbursement is to provide *incentive payments* to pharmacists who meet specific performance goals or engage in certain activities. For instance, a pharmacist might receive an incentive payment if he or she exceeds the target generic dispensing rate in that geographic area. The amount received depends on the pharmacy's generic substitution rate and the total savings from generic dispensing by all network pharmacies. This plan can be expanded to include incentives for switching prescriptions to preferred drugs or performing activities such as patient monitoring or education. Incentive payments are a new phenomenon. Whether they result in better care and patient outcomes and really catch on as a reimbursement method remains to be seen.

Payment for Cognitive Services

Finally, *payment for cognitive services* is another emerging reimbursement method. This is a major issue in pharmaceutical circles as the profession attempts to separate pharmacy payment for the drug product itself from a pharmacist's services in order to ensure that the latter are recognized and valued. These services can include patient counseling and education, drug monitoring and refraining from dispensing an unnecessary prescription.

There is a significant difference between incentive payments (described above) and paying for cognitive services. Incentive payments are made only for services specified by the pharmacy benefits manager, while cognitive services payments are for services identified by the pharmacist as medically necessary for the patient. The pharmacy and payer agree ahead of time on which services are included, and charges are based on utilization.

Evaluating Reimbursement Methods

◐ *Quality of patient care*

◐ *Ease of administration*

◐ *Accountability*

◐ *Cost-effectiveness*

◐ *Accessibility*

◐ *Equity*

Evaluating Reimbursement Methods

In evaluating a pharmacy reimbursement system, there are a number of specific criteria to consider, according to the American Pharmaceutical Association. They include:

Quality of patient care: A reimbursement system should provide incentives for the pharmacist to: (1) improve upon or even ensure the quality of patient care by intervening with the prescriber or patient; (2) avoid underutilization of drug products and cognitive services; and (3) avoid overutilization of drug products and cognitive services.

Ease of administration: A reimbursement system should be: (1) easy and inexpensive for the PBM and participating pharmacies to manage, and (2) easily incorporated into existing claims processing systems.

Accountability: A reimbursement system should contain mechanisms to assure that services are being performed as agreed and that claims are being submitted properly in a timely manner.

Cost-effectiveness: A reimbursement system should provide incentives for the pharmacist to consider both cost and effectiveness when selecting or recommending drug products.

Accessibility: A reimbursement system should encourage pharmacist participation in the network and acceptance of covered patients.

Equity: A reimbursement system should be fair to both the payer and participating pharmacies.

Claims Processing and Point-of-Sale (POS) Technology

Claims processing has changed tremendously in a relatively short time, primarily because of computers. Under the traditional fee-for-service system, a prescription was dispensed, and some time later the plan member submitted a paper claim for payment, often to a third party administrator (TPA) hired by the employer to process claims. Claims that didn't meet the approved criteria were rejected or returned to the plan member for more information. For some time, TPAs continued to handle claims processing alone, though their computer capabilities became increasingly complex and capable of greater speed and efficiency.

When pharmacy benefits management (PBM) companies, which attempt to intervene in prescriber behavior and patient compliance as well as handle claims processing, began proliferating (see Chapters 1 and 8), employers were offered many new services, such as benefit design, data capture and analysis, provider contracting and reimbursement, network management, financial reporting and drug utilization review, among others. Perhaps the biggest leap into the future, however, was the advent of point-of-sale (POS) electronic claims technology, which allows a prescription claim to be processed at the same time the prescription is being dispensed, a system similar to that used during a credit card purchase. A preliminary screening of the claim is done as the prescription is being filled, including checking such factors as whether the drug is covered under the member's health plan and duplicate claims. In some cases, payment can be calculated, too. In addition, messages or warnings (called *edits*) can be sent online, in real time, from the PBM to the pharmacy. For instance, messages related to prospective drug use review or prior authorization requirements can be relayed before the prescription is actually dispensed, catching mistakes and inefficiencies before it's too late.

The capabilities of point-of-service technology can include:[14]
- Verifying patient eligibility
- Determining deductible status
- Conducting prospective drug use review
- Reducing rejected or denied claims
- Adjudicating claims and capturing data
- Reducing prior authorization problems
- Enforcing formularies.

POS technology represents a tremendous advantage to both the pharmacy benefits manager and the participating pharmacy. For the PBM, more complex formulary and prior authorization guidelines can be implemented without unnecessary denial of claims. In other words, real-time messages through the POS can replace claims denial as a means of encouraging providers to implement criteria and guidelines. The amount of paperwork is also greatly reduced. For the pharmacy, claims adjudication and payment are faster and more certain.

While not common yet, point-of-sale connections between the PBM and the prescriber are certainly feasible. This has many important implications for prescribers, pharmacies and benefit managers in making efficient, effective patient care decisions. For instance, formulary and prior authorization restrictions, drug use criteria, and treatment guidelines can be communicated directly to the physician as the prescription is being written. Continuing advances in POS technology are redefining the roles of everyone involved in pharmaceutical decision making.

Defining and Monitoring Pharmacy Quality

How should the pharmacy benefits manager assess and assure the quality of the services provided by pharmacies participating in the network? This issue is especially important for closed networks with relatively few pharmacies because plan members have fewer choices. With open networks, members can express their dissatisfaction with quality, though indirectly, by taking their business away from one pharmacy to another, but this is less feasible with a restricted list of participating pharmacies.

Three dimensions of quality can be measured by the PBM: (1) *structure*, (2) *process* and (3) *outcome*. *Structural elements of quality* relate to the existence of appropriate facilities, equipment and personnel. In assessing the structural aspect of quality, a checklist can be used to determine if certain factors are present. State licensure of pharmacies is based on a structural assessment of aspects of quality such as sufficient space, required equipment, reference books and appropriately trained and credentialed personnel.

Process involves the services provided to plan members in providing pharmaceutical goods and services and exactly how these are provided. That is, were current practice standards followed? For a given plan member, were all necessary services provided, and were they performed correctly? Process indicators are often stated in terms of levels of activity or quantities of services provided—for instance, the percentage of patients who receive specified services.

Ultimately, the purpose of medical services is to positively influence the health status of patients. This, then, is the *outcome* of care. How did pharmaceutical services affect the outcome of the patient's disease treatment? Did the services delivered have a positive impact on the patient's health?

In measuring these three dimensions of quality, the assumption is that structural elements help improve the likelihood that the process of care is appropriate which, in turn, increases the likelihood of improved patient outcomes. However, the links among the three are not absolutely clear. Bad outcomes can and do occur in spite of state-of-the-art processes being performed in the appropriate settings, and good outcomes can occur in spite of inappropriate processes. Therefore, in assessing the quality of network pharmacies, all three aspects need to be measured. Structure is the easiest to measure but the farthest removed from the actual experience of plan members. Process and outcomes are both essential; neither alone gives a complete picture of quality.

Several examples may help clarify these aspects of quality measurement and their use. One is the quality of care provided by a pharmacy before dispensing a prescription (that is, checking the appropriateness of the prescription, etc., during drug use review. This is discussed in detail in Chapter 5). A structural element is whether or not a pharmacy has a computer system that maintains patient drug histories and whether the system has the capability to check prescriptions for appropriate dosing, duplicate prescriptions and possible drug interactions. A process indicator might be the percentage of new prescriptions in which the pharmacist intervenes with the prescriber in some way to improve the quality of therapy.

A second example has to do with the quality of patient counseling. A structural element might be the existence of a quiet, private area where the pharmacist can talk to patients about their drugs. Process might be measured by an indicator such as the percentage of patients with chronic conditions who receive personal counseling about their medications. Intermediate outcomes might be gauged by the percentage of patients who are compliant with drug therapy or the percentage who can pass a short knowledge quiz about their drug (what it's used for, how to take it, etc.). Patient outcomes might be measured by the percentage of patients whose illnesses are under control because (at least partially) of drug therapy.

In terms of other standards for measuring quality, the Omnibus Budget Reconciliation Act of 1990 (OBRA '90) spelled out requirements for pharmacies serving Medicaid patients regarding maintenance of patient profiles, prospective drug use review and patient counseling. These requirements reflect what should be expected of quality network pharmacies in general. According to OBRA '90,[15] in their patient profiles, pharmacists should maintain information on: the patient's disease state(s); the patient's allergies and drug reactions; a comprehensive list of medications and relevant devices used by the patient (such as those used to administer or monitor drugs); and adverse reactions to drug therapy experienced and reported by the patient.

In conducting drug use review before filling a prescription, the pharmacist should screen the prescription for the following potential problems: therapeutic duplications; drug-disease contraindications; drug-drug interactions, including serious interactions with nonprescription products; incorrect drug dose or duration of therapy; drug-allergy interactions; and possible clinical abuse or misuse.

Regarding counseling patients about the drugs dispensed to them, OBRA mandates that the pharmacist must offer to discuss with patients matters that he or she deems significant including: name and description of the medication; dosage form, dosage and duration; special directions and precautions in preparing and administering the medication; common or severe side effects that may occur and actions required if they do occur; techniques for self-monitoring drug therapy; proper storage of medication; refill information; and what to do if a dose is missed.

Note: Appendix 3 is a categorized list of pharmacy performance criteria.

Member Satisfaction

Quality can also be assessed by the plan member in terms of patient satisfaction with pharmacy services. As mentioned earlier, in an open network, patients can express their unhappiness with pharmacy service by taking their business elsewhere, but that's harder to do with a short list of pharmacies. Therefore, an important part of quality assessment is to directly measure patient satisfaction with the pharmacies they are expected to patronize.

Satisfaction with pharmacy services is multidimensional in that various characteristics of the services offered can generate their own levels of satisfaction. To address these different levels, a questionnaire has been developed to measure patient satisfaction with pharmacies.[16] The dimensions it includes are: consideration, explanation, technical competence and general satisfaction. (See Appendix 4 for this instrument.)

Questions to Ask About Network Development

1. What type of network does the PBM use (open or closed)? Are enough pharmacies participating to ensure easy access? Is 24-hour availability provided? Is delivery available?

2. By what reimbursement method are pharmacies paid by the PBM? Are there incentives for pharmacists to perform cognitive services? What behaviors are rewarded and how? Does the payment system promote quality of care? Cost-effectiveness? How?

3. What are the incentives for the pharmacy to dispense generic products?

4. Does the PBM have a MAC program? What is the source of MAC prices? How many drugs are included on the MAC list? What are the criteria for a product to have a MAC? Who is responsible for selecting MAC drugs and assuring the quality of the products? How often is the MAC list updated? Is the PBM willing to provide a periodic report on how much money the MAC saved?

5. Is a point-of-sale (POS) system operational? What are its claims processing capabilities? What are its capabilities for utilization review and other therapy management tools such as formularies and prior authorization?

6. How does the PBM measure quality among participating pharmacies? Does the PBM monitor quality indicators related to structure, process and outcomes? How does the PBM assure quality among par-

ticipating providers? Does the PBM regularly measure patient satisfaction with pharmacies? How?

Endnotes

1. Marion Merrell Dow, *Managed Care Digest*/HMO Edition, 1994, 41.
2. Ibid.
3. B. Watkins, "Changing Channels," *Business & Health Special Report: Managed Care Comes to Prescription Drugs*, 1991, 17.
4. Marion Merrell Dow, *Managed Care Digest*/HMO Edition, 1994, 43-44.
5. "Purchasing Prescription Drug Mail Service Effectively," *Managing Prescription Drug Benefits* (Chicago: Midwest Business Group on Health), 10.
6. Ibid., 15.
7. Ibid.
8. *A New Outpatient Pharmacy Service Benefit: Achieving Value From Pharmacist Services*. (Washington, DC: American Pharmaceutical Association, 1994).
9. "Using MAC Provisions for Cost-Effective Generic Drug Buying," *Managing Prescription Drug Benefits*, 12.
10. "Pharmacy Services in Managed Care," *Medical Interface*, May 1993, 88.
11. R. Navarro, "Capitation Risks for Pharmacy Services," *Medical Interface*, July 1994, 89.
12. "Pharmacy Risk-Sharing Promotes Savings," *Business & Health Special Report: Pharmacy Benefits Management: The Next Generation*, 1995, 19.
13. Ibid.
14. "Medicaid Pharmacy Programs Preparing for Point-of-Sale System," *Medicaid Pharmacy Bulletin* 5 (1) (January-February 1991).
15. W. L. Fitzgerald, "Legal Control of Pharmacy Services," in B. R. Canaday, ed., *OBRA '90: A Practical Guide to Effecting Pharmaceutical Care* (American Pharmaceutical Association, 1994).
16. L. N. Larson and L. D. MacKeigan, "Further Validation of an Instrument to Measure Patient Satisfaction With Pharmacy Services," *Journal of Pharmaceutical Marketing and Management* 8 (1) (1994): 125-139.

Cost Management

○ Aggressiveness of benefit management
○ Physician interaction and education
○ Drug utilization review and formulary capabilities
○ Generic substitution rates achieved
○ Size and stringency of MAC list
○ Impact of MAC provisions and generic discounts on overall costs for your population and the mix of products used

Service

○ Customer service and telephone support resources
○ Turnaround time
○ Shipping capabilities: cool-packs, express delivery
○ Staffing complement, especially for "peak periods"
○ Administrative support to plan, i.e., a dedicated account representative
○ Protocols for working with physicians
○ Availability and expertise of pharmacists

Site Visit

○ Adequacy of physical plant
○ Use of advanced technology such as bar coding, robotics and computerization

○ Match between marketing promises and reality
○ Flexibility and responsiveness to plan needs

Quality Assurance

○ Error rates and prevention procedures
○ Classification and correction of errors
○ Presence of TQM program
○ Billing accuracy

Point of Service and Reporting

○ Ability to process claims online, in real time
○ Integration with retail networks
○ Understandable, useful management reports
○ System backup provisions

◑ Processing mode: real time/online versus
batch updates

◑ Is dispensing, claims payment and eligibility
information immediately available to both
mail and retail?

◑ Level of system flexibility: i.e., can the system
handle variable copays and deductibles?

◑ Experience integrating with specific vendors

◑ System backup and emergency provisions

◑ Useful reporting with appropriate information
about mail, retail and integrated performance

◑ Vendor capability to provide total clinical and
financial management of the overall benefit

◑ Relationship between mail and retail vendors:
i.e., owned, subcontracted, independent

◑ System integration should be "transparent" to
both the plan and members.

◑ Time lag between eligibility and dispensing
in filling mail scripts

Pharmacy Performance Criteria

Quality Factors

- Access: hours, location(s), delivery
- Physical plant: cleanliness, counseling space
- Financial viability
- Dispensing practices conform to professional standards
- Handling of controlled substances
- Online computer capabilities
- Status with licensure board
- Staffing standards: type and quantity of staff, performance standards, training, use of technicians
- Quantity and variety of inventory
- Procedure for handling complaints
- Quality management and improvement programs
- Counseling consistency and quality
- Auditing type and frequency

Contract Compliance/Fraud and Abuse

- Compliance with all contract terms
- Full documentation: online, paper prescriptions, signature logs
- DAW (dispense as written): correct codes for each claim, documentation of physician contact where appropriate
- Usual and customary rate given when lower than discounted (contractual) rate
- Refills: correct quantity actually dispensed

◑ Patient actually receives drug
◑ Product billed for is dispensed (i.e., brand versus generic)
◑ DUR performance: Are pharmacists acting on items such as allergies, drug interactions, failure to refill?

Appendix 4 . . .
Patient Satisfaction With Pharmacy Services Questionnaire

Respond to each statement with the appropriate number:

Strongly Agree	Agree	Not Sure	Disagree	Strongly Disagree
1	2	3	4	5

Consideration

The pharmacist spends as much time
as is necessary with me.   _____

My prescriptions are always filled promptly.   _____

Sometimes the pharmacist does not spend
enough time with me.   _____

The pharmacy staff should be more friendly.   _____

The pharmacist should do more to keep people
from having problems with their medications.   _____

I usually have to wait a long time when I get
a prescription filled.   _____

The pharmacy staff seem to have a genuine
interest in me as a person.   _____

The pharmacy staff are always courteous
and respectful.   _____

Explanation

The pharmacist usually explains the possible side
effects that a new medication may cause.   _____

If I have a question about my prescription,
the pharmacist is always available to help me.   _____

The pharmacist knows how to explain things
in a way that I understand. _____

When I get a prescription filled, the pharmacist makes
sure that I understand how to take the medication. _____

The pharmacist hardly ever explains what
the medication does. _____

The pharmacist often does not tell me how to take
my prescription medication. _____

Technical Competence

The pharmacist isn't as thorough as he or she could be. _____

I am confident that the pharmacist dispenses
all prescriptions correctly. _____

I sometimes wonder about the accuracy of the
prescriptions that the pharmacist dispenses. _____

The pharmacist is always thorough. _____

General Satisfaction

The pharmacy services that I've received
are just about perfect. _____

There are things about my pharmacy services that I
receive that could be better. _____

I have some complaints about the pharmacy services. _____

I'm very satisfied with the pharmacy services
that I receive. _____

This chapter discusses the formulary, a critical component in a managed pharmacy benefits plan. A *formulary* is a list of the drugs considered by the pharmacy benefits manager to be those most useful in patient care, rated on the basis of clinical effectiveness and cost. According to the American Society of Hospital Pharmacists (ASHP), the purpose of the formulary is to improve the quality of patient care and control costs through the rational selection and use of drugs. At their best, formularies promote appropriate prescribing, establish a common standard of practice and contribute to outcomes research.

Formularies are quite variable in nature, but there are two main types. *Open formularies* typically list a large number of products, and new drugs are fairly easily added. Prescribers are encouraged but not required to choose drugs from this list. Most drugs, whether on the formulary or not (with the possible exception of those exclusions explained in Chapter 2), are covered under the member's plan.

Chapter 4...

Formularies

Closed, or restricted, formularies list only a limited number of products and are very selective in adding new drugs. Physicians may have to prescribe from this list for a drug to be covered under the member's pharmacy benefit plan. Sometimes degrees of coverage are involved. According to the Marion Merrell Dow, *Managed Care Digest*/HMO Edition, 1994, a closed formulary commonly requires prior authorization by the PBM for coverage of nonformulary drugs.

Formularies are also sometimes classified as *limited* formularies, which restrict the number of drugs permitted in each therapeutic class, and *unlimited*, which have no such restrictions. In a limited formulary, the addition of a new drug requires the deletion of one already on the list. Combinations of formularies are not uncommon. For example, a formulary may be both closed and limited.

The percentage of HMOs using drug formularies rose to 76% during 1993, the highest level ever. HMOs with formularies covered 40.5 million enrollees or 85% of all HMO members in 1993, up from 76% and 32.2 million in 1992. Staff and group HMOs were the most likely HMO models to use formularies. Three-fourths of HMOs with formularies used open formularies in 1993. The oldest HMOs were most likely to have formularies, and the use of these lists increased with the size of the HMO.[1]

Of the 76% of HMOs that used formularies in 1993, nearly three-fourths included at least 500 drugs. HMOs with formularies reported filling 87% of prescriptions using formulary drugs.[2]

The formulary began in hospital pharmacies. In fact, more than 25 years ago, the Joint Commission on Accreditation of Healthcare Organizations (JCAHO) mandated formulary development for hospitals. They were originally developed to avoid overstocking hospital pharmacy inventories and to keep costs lower by using less expensive drugs.[3]

Formularies are relatively easy to develop and enforce in clearly structured, integrated health care facilities like hospitals and HMOs, where physicians and pharmacists work in close physical proximity and communication is generally good. In contrast, today's pharmacy benefits manager may work with a loosely aligned and far-flung network of pharmacies and numerous prescribers who work independently of the PBM.

This disadvantage is somewhat offset by recent advances in information processing such as point-of-service (POS) capabilities and communications technology. (See Chapter 3 for more on this topic.) POS technology allows real-time communication between the PBM and pharmacy as prescriptions are being filled. For instance, warning messages can be transmit-

---

Characteristics of an Effective Formulary

The characteristics of an effective formulary include the following: [4]

- ◐ *It specifies drugs of choice based on safety and efficacy.*

- ◐ *It includes second-line alternatives where needed.*

- ◐ *It keeps therapeutic duplication to a minimum by excluding duplicative or inferior products.*

- ◐ *It considers the ratio of benefits to cost.*

ted to the pharmacy at the time a prescription is being dispensed to alert the pharmacist as to whether a drug is on the formulary or to advise about prior authorization requirements. In addition, advanced computer capabilities now mean that formularies can be customized to meet the needs of local areas. This feature facilitates participation in formulary decision making by local leaders in medicine and pharmacy. In short, techniques and tools that were previously limited to organizations with integrated medical staffs can now be used in less structured managed care organizations (MCOs) with scattered providers.

Developing the Formulary

Persuading prescribers to accept and follow the formulary is critical if the formulary is to influence prescribing patterns, contain costs and improve the quality of patient care. Regardless of how scientifically sound the formulary may be, if it's not accepted by plan physicians as legitimate, it won't be followed. Therefore, the process of formulary development can be as important as the final product.

The method of evaluating and selecting drugs for the formulary is called the *formulary system*.[5] The operational characteristics of a well-designed formulary include:[6]

- ◑ The content of the formulary is determined by a representative committee that includes knowledgeable physicians and pharmacists, generally called a P&T (pharmacy and therapeutics) committee.
- ◑ Decisions to add and delete products are based on scientific information.
- ◑ New drugs on the market are added when evidence of unique therapeutic contribution is accumulated.
- ◑ Communications support the goal that practicing physicians and pharmacists understand the formulary.
- ◑ The formulary receives adequate administrative support.

As mentioned above, in managed health care plans, formularies are generally developed by P&T committees comprised of physicians and pharmacists with extensive experience and knowledge of both the clinical and economic sides of pharmacy. Some committees also include a pharmacy director, medical director, purchasing director, quality assurance manager and physician specialists. Because certain specialists such as those in family practice, internal medicine, pediatrics and OB/GYN prescribe most medications, they often serve on these committees. Members agree to abide by standards of ethical conduct, including the disclosure of potential conflicts of interest.

Formulary decisions made by the P&T committee are based on scientific data gleaned from both medical literature and clinical experience. Committees typically consider five major issues when evaluating formulary products for possible inclusion:[7]

Therapeutic appropriateness for a specific condition. For instance, many doctors consider diet pills inappropriate therapy for obesity so would not include them on a managed health plan's formulary.

Uniqueness. P&T committees determine if any of their patients would benefit from a particular product alone, and not any other. For this reason, they avoid most *me-too* drugs, the name given to pharmaceuticals that offer little or no therapeutic gain over existing drugs.

Clinical experience. Members may assess peer-reviewed papers to evaluate a drug's performance in clinical trials or talk to other MCOs that have used it. They may also use various guidelines established by medical societies and expert panels.

Product future. Committees evaluate a product's clinical and economic future, considering products still in the development stage that might make the drug under consideration obsolete. They also note the time left until a drug's patent expires and generic versions might be available.

Cost. Short-term product costs such as staff education, laboratory tests and followup office visits, and long-term issues such as likely cost increases or decreases are assessed.

Formulary Composition

Formularies are usually published both in book form (some running several hundred pages long) and as an electronic database. Individual drugs may be ranked with from one to five dollar sign symbols, from "most effective, greatest cost benefit ($) to least effective, least cost benefit ($$$$$)." On some formularies, dollar signs represent price levels only. Drugs judged as too expensive or not effective enough are not placed on the list at all.

Typical formularies now contain between 1,000 and 1,200 drugs.[8] However, most experts expect that number to decline dramatically. In fact, some observers think formularies will eventually disappear altogether. Based on extensive research with more than 50 pharmaceutical and biotechnology companies, one PBM industry executive estimated that by the year 2005 virtually all health plans will have extremely restricted formularies, containing only about 300 drugs, compared to approximately 4,000 today.[9] If this prediction is accurate, it's clearly an indication that the drugs that survive must offer unprecedented effectiveness, safety and economy.

Formulary drugs may be under one of four classifications: (1) *unrestricted*, (2) *monitored*, (3) *restricted* or (4) *conditional*. An *unrestricted* medication may be prescribed freely, without the prescriber having to ask anyone's permission. A *monitored* classification usually indicates that the drug in question may be prescribed only after the case has been reviewed by another plan physician or group of physicians. A classification of *restricted* usually indicates that a medication may be prescribed only by certain doctors or only for certain medical conditions. A *conditional* drug is one that's available on the formulary only for a certain amount of time as a trial period.[10]

An alternative or complement to formularies is *prior authorization*, which requires approval from the PBM before a prescription can be dispensed as a covered service. The authorization may be initiated by the prescribing physician or by the dispensing pharmacy; usually it's the latter. Sometimes time limits are placed on responding to the request. For example, if no response is received within 48 hours, the request is assumed to be approved. Generally, prior authorization is used in conjunction with prescribing criteria for drugs that are expensive, potentially toxic or effective in well-defined but limited cases.

According to the ASHP, a formulary should also contain "important ancillary information." For example, the formulary published by PCS Health Systems, a leading PBM company, is organized by disease states and drug classes. Each section contains:
- A few general facts about the drug class
- A list of available drug products
- The relative cost of each drug
- Whether the product is prescription or nonprescription
- Whether the product is available generically.

Formulary Drug Selection

A formulary is based on the premise that among similar drugs, some are better than others. The better drug may be more effective, for example, have fewer side effects, be less expensive or have a more convenient dosing schedule, which helps with patient compliance. Whatever the reason or combination of reasons, one or more drugs are preferred over similar products, and these drugs are awarded a place on the formulary, a status much sought after by pharmaceutical manufacturers.

Before P&T committees select these preferred products, decisions must be made as to which drugs can be substituted for certain others. In other words, what drugs are considered to be clinically equivalent?

Defining equivalent drugs is a very important part of formulary management leading to choices of preferred drugs within a group of equivalent or "substitutable" products. Once the drugs of choice are selected, guidelines can be developed for substitution and interchange, when a drug is switched from the one initially prescribed to one that is preferred because of its therapeutic superiority and/or lower cost. Therapeutic interchange typically involves substituting such products with the consent of the prescriber.

Therapeutic alternates are defined as different chemical entities that can be expected to have similar effects on patients in terms of health outcomes. These products may be members of the same therapeutic class. Determining therapeutic equivalence is fairly subjective because no test or measurement instrument exists.

The designation of therapeutic alternates is the cornerstone of activities geared to influence the cost of pharmaceutical care. Once products are designated as therapeutic alternates, price can then play a role in selecting from among preferred products. To illustrate, let's assume that a P&T committee designates several products in a particular class as therapeutically interchangeable. Because they are "equal," price can be considered in choosing the preferred products. If, however, a drug is deemed to be "in a class by itself," or without therapeutic alternates, then its price is less relevant in formulary decisions.

In closed formulary systems such as hospitals, protocols may be developed so that therapeutic substitution is done automatically based on the physician's approval of the protocol itself rather than individual approval for each patient or drug. In more open systems like pharmacy networks, other means of implementation are used. Provider education programs, for example, may be designed to promote preferred products. Pharmacies can also be encouraged to try to get the prescriber to switch to the preferred drug. The important point is that such activities first require that these products are designated as therapeutic alternates.

Generic Substitution

Bioequivalent products are equal, pharmaceutically speaking, in that they have the same active ingredient(s), strength and dosage form. As noted in Chapter 3, the FDA evaluates bioequivalence and publishes the results in *Approved Drug Products With Therapeutic Equivalence* Evaluations, or what is more commonly called the *Orange Book*, a comprehensive reference often used by PBMs in selecting the products that are subject to the requirements and incentives for generic substitution.

Bioequivalent drugs also must have similar *bioavailability*, which refers to the rate and extent of the drug's absorption in the body. The substitution of one bioequivalent product for another is called *generic substitution*. Generics are drugs labeled with a chemical name rather than a brand or trade name that have been on the market long enough that the original manufacturer no longer has patent protection, and the drugs are available from multiple sources. Increasing the use of generic equivalents is an especially important formulary cost-management strategy. Generics nearly always cost substantially less than the equivalent brand-name drugs–about half as much on average, according to the Generic Pharmaceutical Association. That makes them especially attractive to patients.

According to one source, dispensing a generic in place of a brand-name drug can mean a $15 to $20 difference in cost to the patient for a 30-day supply. As a rule of thumb, increasing the generic substitution rate 5% will reduce the total cost of drugs to the health plan by 15% to 20%.[11]

Generic substitution was required by 73% of HMOs in 1993, up from 70% in 1992. The practice affected 34.1 million HMO enrollees. HMOs that were at least 15 years old (80% of them) were more inclined to require generic drug substitution.[12]

The practice of generic substitution is governed by state drug product selection laws. Incentives may be used to persuade physicians, pharmacists and patients to use generics. However, not everyone is enthusiastic about using generics in place of branded products, especially brand-name pharmaceutical manufacturers and some physicians. Manufacturers object on the grounds that brand names are more expensive because research costs must be recouped, and they often believe they are clinically more effective as well. This view, however, is disputed by many experts, including the FDA.

One of the ways pharmaceutical firms try to persuade physicians to prescribe their brand-name products rather than generic equivalents is through a process called *detailing*, or marketing specific drugs through person-to-person office visits by sales representatives. (Detailing is also used for educational and other purposes.) According to a study by Foster Higgins, drug companies spend a total of $2.5 billion annually on marketing, which translates to approximately $5,000 for every doctor in the United States.[13] Manufacturers defend detailing, saying it's as much about education as it is marketing, and that drug company sales representatives, who know the products well, are best suited to educate physicians about particular products.

In addition to manufacturers' objections, some physicians protest required generic substitution because they feel the practice interferes with the doctor/patient relationship, as well as with the doctor's right to choose from among available medications. Physicians' negativity about the issue of generic substitution may vary with their own degree of financial risk. In some health plans, doctors pay for the drugs they prescribe out of a risk pool of funds. They may keep any unspent money, a financial incentive that can encourage them to prescribe generic products more often.

Managing the Formulary

The P&T committee is responsible for managing and maintaining the formulary and evaluating the clinical use of drugs, as well as handling other policies, procedures and programs to improve the quality of drug therapy.

Several activities are important in maintaining a formulary and continually improving its effectiveness. The *process* of refining or changing the formulary should be described formally through published policies and procedures. These documents explain the process of routine formulary maintenance through regular reviews and updates, the process of requesting changes in the formulary, and the steps necessary to make additions, deletions or changes. Because formulary development involves human judgment and therefore is somewhat subjective, the process of *how* formulary decisions are made is critical in assessing the quality of the formulary. The decision making process can enhance or diminish the credibility of a formulary and the likelihood that it will be used as intended.

Two primary elements of formulary maintenance are *therapeutic drug class reviews* and *drug monographs*. Both deal with the acquisition and presentation of the scientific and clinical information used in formulary decision making. Therapeutic drug class reviews are formal evaluations of the available clinical evidence necessary to identify preferred drugs within a therapeutic class. The reviews include both scientific evidence and P&T committee member input. They should be done on an ongoing basis, so that selected drugs are reviewed each year. These reviews may result in changes to the formulary, new or revised drug use criteria, or treatment guidelines.

As part of the process of making an addition or deletion of an individual drug to the formulary, an evaluation report, or *monograph*, of the drug being considered for formulary addition or deletion should be prepared. This monograph presents a thorough synopsis of the research and clinical literature that's available on the drug.

Enforcing the Formulary

A formulary is effective only if it's used by prescribers in daily practice, that is, if physicians prescribe formulary drugs. How do managed care organizations enforce their formularies and promote their use in day-to-day decision making?

Hospitals and HMOs with their own in-house pharmacies are similar in that they are fairly integrated, and the medical staff is part of the organizational structure. Therefore, they can establish administrative policies and procedures to govern the use of nonformulary drugs. For instance, special forms and procedures for requesting and/or justifying the use of a nonformulary drug can be required. In some cases, the medical staff, through the P&T committee, can implement therapeutic interchange protocols that allow the pharmacy to dispense a product other than the one prescribed. Even among integrated systems, though, the enforcement of the formulary can vary greatly. Some may be very strict, while others are lax.

In less integrated systems, such as a PBM company working with a network of community pharmacies with no organizational links to prescribers, administrative or regulatory enforcement strategies can be more difficult to implement. However, other methods are available, such as the use of a closed formulary. In Medicaid programs, for instance, only formulary products are covered.

Another strategy is to pay the pharmacist a fee for getting the prescriber to change a prescription from a nonformulary to a formulary drug. This practice is controversial among practicing pharmacists unless the switch can be justified on therapeutic grounds. If the switch is seen as a cost-containment tactic that may not be in the patient's best interest, the practice may be subject to criticism. The problem is intensified if the formulary (or switching drugs to formulary products) is seen as a marketing device to promote the sale of a particular manufacturer's products.

Finally, the formulary can be implemented by educating prescribers to encourage them to comply with its recommendations. For the PBM in a loosely integrated system of providers, the formulary is better viewed as an educational, rather than a regulatory, tool. Since the formulary is presumed to reflect current clinical judgment, noncompliance can be seen as a need for education. The formulary compliance of individual providers can be monitored through physician and pharmacy profiles, using indicators such as "percent of prescriptions for nonformulary products." Prescribers or pharmacists who are not compliant with formulary drugs can be targeted for educational materials or in-person visits. The formulary can be detailed, much like drug manufacturers detail their products, as described earlier. This type of education should be ongoing, with a focus on reinforcing appropriate clinical strategies. Successful programs combine phone calls to change specific drugs, physician profiling to target formulary outliers and unbiased educational material, seminars and lectures. Information can also be transmitted electronically.

It's an increasing practice for PBMs to detail doctors directly. One large PBM, for instance, monitors physicians' prescribing habits, then writes or calls them if their prescriptions deviate significantly from the norm. Another employs pharmacist telemarketers who call physicians and ask them to switch mail-order prescriptions to generics or preferred drugs.[14]

The Economics of Formularies and Rebates

Pharmacy expenditures are a function of the products used and the price and quantity of these products, all of which can be influenced by a formulary. Formularies can reduce the cost of products in at least four ways:

1. They can reduce inefficient utilization by not recommending products that are more expensive but no more effective than others (the therapeutic alternates).

2. A second way is by reducing inventory costs. For HMOs with in-house pharmacies (or with hospitals), the entity that develops the formulary is also the one that buys drugs from manufacturers or wholesalers. In these systems, a formulary represents a reduction in inventory costs because fewer products are purchased. For instance, if six products are thought to be similar, and two are selected for the HMO's formulary, the other four need not be on the shelf. This is not the case in fee-for-service plans. Here the organization buys prescriptions from pharmacies that serve many other clients, and they probably need to keep all six products available.

3. The third—and more direct—way in which formularies can reduce the price of products is for the PBM to use the formulary as a bargaining tool to *negotiate special contract pieces from manufacturers*. In such an arrangement, the manufacturer is willing to reduce its unit price in exchange for increased market share or sales volume. Basically, the reduced price is the concession given by the manufacturer for the higher sales resulting from the PBM's formulary recommendations.

4. *Rebates*, another formulary price reduction tool, work this way: A drug manufacturer pays a rebate to the PBM based on the volume of its products that were used or sold through the PBM. Re-

bates are calculated as a percentage of the amount paid to pharmacies by the PBM for claims involving the manufacturer's products (in other words, the total ingredient cost of the manufacturer's products paid to pharmacies). The rebate might be a flat percentage of the manufacturer's sales that go through the PBM, or it might be tied to performance requirements where the size of the rebate is dependent upon the quantity of the manufacturer's products distributed through the PBM. In this case, the PBM is rewarded if it can increase use of the drug company's products. The rebates received by a PBM for the drugs used by a particular payer are reported to that payer and the money is divided between them. The proportion going to each party is spelled out in their contractual agreement.

These practices are controversial because of this question: What is the primary purpose of the formulary—cost control or improved patient care? The problem is that these two aspects are difficult to separate, since value (the relationship between benefit and price) is a criterion that is used legitimately in making formulary decisions. The issue becomes even more convoluted as ties between many PBMs and manufacturers grow closer through the numerous mergers and acquisitions that have occurred recently. The issue becomes: Is the formulary a statement of clinical preferences, or is it a tool to market drugs from particular manufacturers? (Chapter 8 has more information on PBM/drug company alliances.)

Are formularies as cost-effective as they're supposed to be? Although some studies have not shown that formularies save money, most practitioners currently think they do. But just how much is difficult to say because formularies and drug benefit plan designs vary so much. One PBM, however, estimates that an open formulary can save from 3% to 4% the first year, and as much as 7% to 10% in subsequent years.[15] A recent study demonstrated that hospitals using a formulary and therapeutic interchange spend 13.4% less for drugs per patient day than hospitals that do not use either strategy.[16]

The Future of Formularies

Those who develop formularies should guard against becoming too restrictive, a situation that can have negative consequences for patients, physicians, pharmacists and payers. An emerging problem as formularies become more numerous and complicated is that most physicians now participate in multiple managed care plans, each with its own (often very different) formulary. There has been speculation that in these cases most doctors prescribe according to the most restrictive formulary, and the use of multiple formularies may unintentionally limit patient access to the most appropriate medication. A study of this prescribing behavior conducted on behalf of the American Association of Preferred Provider Organizations (AAPPO) and the National Pharmaceutical Council (NPC) found that restrictive formularies may indeed have a negative impact on physician prescribing.[17] Another study sponsored by the NPC found a correlation between high restriction of pharmaceutical choices and subsequent higher medical costs in four different diagnoses.[18] Similar studies have shown the same relationship.

In the future, indications are that formulary drugs will be selected on a more scientific and less subjective basis than they are now, relying on outcomes research currently being conducted. The ideal formulary should not simply limit drug choices but be the basis for clinical guidelines and treatment protocols. One PBM's formulary, for instance, discusses the differences among drugs in a particular therapeutic class and offers guidelines on how those drugs should be prescribed.[19]

Another PBM has organized its formulary by disease states to provide detailed suggestions on standards of care. One of those protocols is *step (or stepped) therapy*, which allows physicians and/or pharmacists to prescribe or dispense more expensive drugs only after they have tried less costly treatments or products. (Some MCOs allow pharmacists to implement step therapy after they have obtained authorization from the prescribing physician.) For example, for hypertension, the formulary guidelines suggest nondrug treatments such as exercise, weight loss and salt restriction for the first three to six months, then diuretics, then a beta blocker drug, but only if the less expensive and invasive treatments haven't worked.[20]

The formulary's ultimate goal, according to most experts, is to serve as an easy-to-use reference for physicians in prescribing medications. This resource might take an electronic form through a desktop computer or a hand-held device. Eventually, technology will allow formulary guidelines to be integrated with a patient's medical records and drug history, so that doctors can easily select not just the most cost-effective drug, but the one that will work best for that particular patient.[21]

Questions to Ask About Formularies

1. Does the PBM have a formulary? Is it open or closed? Limited or unlimited?

2. Does the formulary contain information beyond a list of drugs? What information?

3. Is the formulary easy to use?

4. How are deviations from the formulary handled (differential copay, etc.)?

5. Does the PBM have policies and procedures for maintaining the formulary? Who is responsible for formulary decisions? Are there regular reviews of drug classes? Are there formal procedures for adding or deleting a drug? Are monographs prepared?

6. Does the PBM have a pharmacy and therapeutics (P&T) committee? What are its responsibilities? What are the credentials of its members? Are members required to sign a conflict-of-interest statement?

7. Is formulary compliance of individual providers monitored? What means are used to improve compliance with the formulary (incentive payments, education program, etc.)?

8. Is therapeutic interchange encouraged? By what means is it encouraged? Who decides what drugs are therapeutically equivalent?

9. What is the PBM's policy on generic substitution?

10. Does the PBM have rebate agreements with some manufacturers? What is the agreement based on? What is the potential savings?

11. Is prior authorization required for certain drugs? Which drugs or situations require prior approval? Who develops the criteria for authorization decisions? Who makes the approval/disapproval decision?

Endnotes

1. Marion Merrell Dow, *Managed Care Digest*/HMO Edition, 1994, 46-47.
2. Ibid.
3. K. Chitwood, B. Edgren and N. Schultz, "Drug Formularies," *Medical Interface*, December 1993, 72.
4. T. D. Rucker and G. Schiff, "Drug Formularies: Myths in Formation," *Medical Care* 28 (1990): 928-942.
5. "ASHP Guidelines on Formulary System Management," *American Journal of Hospital Pharmacy* 49 (1992): 648-652.
6. Rucker and Schiff, "Drug Formularies."
7. "How P&T Committees Make Decisions," *The Managed Health Care Handbook*, 5-14.
8. "Formularies: Balancing Cost and Quality," *Business & Health Special Report: Pharmacy Benefits Management: The Next Generation* (1995), 26.
9. Interview with Ed Marro, President, MedXL, May 15, 1995.
10. "Integrating a Pharmacy Benefit Program Into a Managed Healthcare Plan" (Chicago: American Association of Preferred Provider Organizations, 1991), 10.
11. "Managing Prescription Drug Benefits"(Chicago: Business Group on Health), 11.
12. Marion Merrell Dow, *Managed Care Digest*/HMO Edition, 1994, 51.

13. "Putting the Squeeze on Drug Benefits Costs," *Business & Health Special Report: Managed Care Comes to Prescription Drugs*, 1991, 10.

14. "Formularies: Balancing Cost and Quality," 25.

15. "Managing Prescription Drug Benefits," 13.

16. T. K. Hazlet and T. W. Hu, "Association Between Formulary Strategies and Hospital Drug Expenditures," *American Journal of Hospital Pharmacy* 49 (1992): 2207-2210.

17. A. Haymes, "Prescribing Behavior of Physicians Utilizing Multiple Formularies." Presentation at the annual AAPPO Fall Forum, Phoenix, AZ, September 1991.

18. "Formularies: Balancing Cost and Quality," 26.

19. Ibid., 27.

20. Ibid.

21. Ibid.

rug utilization review (DUR), a system for monitoring use and improving quality in the delivery of prescription drugs, is a cornerstone of the managed pharmacy benefits program. Studies show that when drug benefits are managed properly, savings on other medical benefits can be significant. DUR can be difficult to implement, and there are some important caveats, but it's an essential component in controlling the utilization of drugs by health plan beneficiaries as well as influencing physician prescribing patterns.

There are several different types of reviews currently in use, but they all have either one or both of the following objectives: (1) to determine drug utilization patterns and cost data, then provide information in an organized format to payers, prescribers and pharmacists; and (2) to establish drug use standards and measure quality according to those standards.

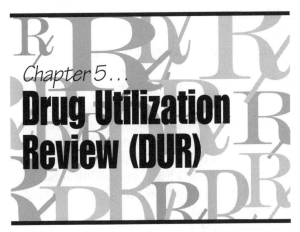

Chapter 5...
Drug Utilization Review (DUR)

DUR helps control costs by:

◑ Decreasing the number of prescriptions that aren't indicated

◑ Reducing inappropriate drug use

◑ Persuading noncompliant physicians to conform to plan guidelines.

This chapter is divided into two main sections: Drug Utilization Review and Utilization Reports (often based on the data derived from DUR).

Drug Utilization Review: An Overview

Following are brief definitions of the basic terms in DUR. All are discussed in more detail later in this chapter.

There are three basic kinds of review:
- Drug utilization review (DUR)
- Drug regimen review (DRR)
- Drug use evaluation (DUE).

The most basic type of review, the *drug utilization review (DUR)*, is typically an audit that provides quantitative feedback to the PBM on plan subscriber drug use. A DUR might supply some or all of the following information:[1]

- Total number of doses per day/duration of therapy
- Method of administration
- Quantity of medication
- Cost of medication
- Appropriateness of medication
- Under- or overutilization
- Laboratory tests performed before and during therapy
- Interactions and abuse
- Adverse reactions to medications
- Duplicate therapies.

A second type is a *drug regimen review (DRR)*, where the focus is on the identification of inappropriate or potentially harmful drug therapy. DRRs have been used for several decades in hospitals and long-term care facilities like nursing homes to identify those cases where patients' drug regimens do not fit their conditions or medical problems, or where duplicative (duplicate) therapy may be present.

A third type, a *drug use evaluation (DUE)*, is a quality assessment review of drug utilization that uses continuous quality improvement (CQI), a common business management tool. Note that the word *evaluation* suggests a judgment regarding quality. CQI is based on the belief that improved systems and processes will reduce the number of undesirable outcomes. With that goal, DUEs establish qualitative standards for drug use in order to ensure safe, effective and appropriate therapy in a cost-effective manner.

Note: Because the terms *DUR, DRR* and *DUE* are sometimes mistakenly used interchangeably, some of the professional literature dealing with different types of drug utilization review systems is confusing. There *are* differences among the terms, as illustrated above. In this discussion, though, the acronym DUR will be used either in reference to the specific quantitative review just described, or when the term is meant generically to indicate a review of drug utilization in general.

Timing

Another important area in DURs relates to their timing. There are three categories of DUR timing: (1) *Prospective DUR* occurs, or at least is initiated, before drug therapy is begun (that is, before the prescription is dispensed); (2) *concurrent DUR* takes place while the therapy is in progress; and (3) *retrospective DUR* is conducted after the drug therapy is completed, or at least a substantial period of time after the therapy is initiated.

There are three timing categories for drug utilization reviews: prospective, concurrent and retrospective.

Focus

A utilization review can focus on one of three areas:
- *Prescribing profiles* of plan physicians
- A particular *drug* or *drug class*
- An individual *patient's drug therapy*.

Why Is DUR So Important?

What has been called the "80/20 rule" appears to hold true when prescription drug benefits are analyzed. In most companies, 80%

In most companies, 80% of prescription claims are filed by just 20% of employees.

of prescription claims are filed by only 20% of employees.[2] This has several implications. One is that 20% of employees take 80% of all the medication dispensed, so the likelihood of inappropriate prescriptions, side effects, allergic reactions, drug interactions and other costly problems increases proportionately in this relatively small group. A more optimistic implication, though, is that DUR is uniquely able to target this high-use, high-risk population so that steps can be taken to control their utilization and, therefore, the company's cost.

Statistics tell the story of why drug utilization review is critically important, especially in managed care. One managed care organization executive believes that two-thirds of the rising cost of drug benefits relates to increased utilization, inappropriate use and the high cost of new drugs.[3] Another source notes that recent studies have documented that between 20% and 40% of all prescriptions are inappropriate in various patient populations.[4] Another estimates that 7% of all hospital admissions are due to drug interactions.[5]

Companies with a high proportion of retirees have reason to be especially concerned about the cost of drug benefits and, consequently, DUR. In some large companies, retirees outnumber active employees by as much as four to one, and retiree drugs can cost as much as 30% to 40% of the total retiree medical plan.[6]

> *Two-thirds of rising drug benefit costs may be related to increased utilization, inappropriate use and the expense of new drugs.*

Drug-related medical problems for retirees increase proportionate to their use. In fact, some studies show that more than 40% of all prescribing for people over age 65 is inappropriate, and one-fourth of all hospitalizations for this age group are related to noncompliance with a drug therapy or to adverse drug reactions.[7] These statistics—prime targets of DUR—are likely to increase as the country's population ages because older people tend to use more drugs—and take them more often—than younger people. Since physicians rarely have expertise in pharmaceuticals, a PBM with a good DUR program can play an important part in helping doctors choose the right drugs for their patients.

DUR is also critical in preventing, identifying and correcting *drug misadventures*, a term that refers to errors in ordering, transcribing, dispensing and administering drugs, as well as to adverse drug reactions. Data presented at the first interdisciplinary conference on drug misadventures indicates that adverse drug events may be costing the United States as much as $100 billion annually,[8] in other words, more than the cost of drugs themselves! One study showed that adverse drug events add approximately $8,000 to a patient's hospital bill.[9] Evidence also indicates that the pharmacist link in the dispensing chain appears to be the strongest, with 70% of the errors occurring either in the ordering or the administration (versus the dispensing) stage.[10]

The History of DURs

The concept that the utilization of prescription drugs should be reviewed and that compiled data should be compared against a set of established standards was born around 1960. DURs caught on in hospitals, which by the 1970s were required to obtain certification from the Joint Commission on Accreditation of Healthcare Organizations (JCAHO). Today, the JCAHO still requires that drug use in health care facilities be monitored and compared to quality standards.[11]

A second major DUR method was mandated by the Omnibus Budget Reconciliation Act of 1990 (OBRA '90) for Medicaid agencies, but the system was quickly adopted by a number of third party payers.[12]

The philosophy of monitoring and measuring the quantity and quality of prescription drug utilization is a perfect fit with managed care. But as managed care evolves and becomes more complex, both the JCAHO and OBRA DUR models have had to be adapted and expanded to meet the changing needs of various health care organizations and administrators.

> *The philosophy of monitoring and measuring the quantity and quality of prescription drug utilization is a perfect fit with managed care.*

How Prevalent Are DUR Programs?

DUR programs are quickly becoming managed care standards. In fact, 62% of HMOs had a formal DUR program in 1993.[13] Of those, 72% extended the program to all prescription drugs. Seventy-one percent of all HMO members were enrolled in plans requiring DUR. Total enrollment in HMOs requiring DUR reached 32.2 million, up 23% from 26.2 million in 1992, and up 69% from 15.5 million in 1991.[14]

Fifty-one percent of HMOs with formal DUR programs named drugs over a certain cost as a criterion for DUR, up dramatically from 24% in 1992. The average cutoff cost was $194.25 per prescription, slightly lower than $198.84 in 1992. The drug cost ceiling used to trigger DUR ranged from a low of $50 per prescription to a high of $600. Staff model HMOs had the lowest ceiling of any model type, at $62.50 per prescription.[15]

The Basic Drug Utilization Review

The American Medical Association (AMA), the American Pharmaceutical Association (APA) and the Pharmaceutical Research and Manufacturers of America (PhRMA) have jointly adopted the following seven principles of DUR:[16]

- ❍ The primary emphasis of a DUR program must be to enhance quality of care for patients by assuring appropriate drug therapy.
- ❍ Criteria and standards for DUR must be clinically relevant.
- ❍ Criteria and standards for DUR must be nonproprietary and must be developed and revised through an open professional consensus process.
- ❍ Interventions must focus on improving therapeutic outcomes.
- ❍ Confidentiality of the relationship between patients and practitioners must be protected.
- ❍ Principles of DUR must apply to the full range of DUR activities, including prospective, concurrent and retrospective drug use evaluation.

◑ DUR program operations must be structured to achieve the principles of DUR.

The Five Steps of DUR

1. Define appropriate drug use in terms of standards.
2. Measure actual use.
3. Compare actual use to standards.
4. Take corrective action.
5. Evaluate impact of DUR on drug utilization patterns.

A DUR program typically involves five elements or steps.[17] The first is to *define appropriate or optimal drug use* in terms of objective and measurable criteria, or standards. These standards become the operational definition of quality.

There are two types of criteria used: *diagnosis criteria* and *drug-specific criteria*.[18] Diagnosis criteria specify the illnesses or types of patients for which a drug should be used, while drug-specific criteria indicate the appropriate doses, durations and other characteristics specific to the use of a certain drug.

The second DUR step is to *measure actual drug use*. This is usually accomplished by using data derived from prescription drug claims as well as patients' drug histories on file with their pharmacies. Data from physician claims may also be available in some systems.

The third element or step in the DUR process is to *compare actual use* against the standards of appropriate use. This step identifies real or potential problems in a patient's therapy or in a physician's prescribing patterns. It assesses the current level of quality by comparing actual practice with the most desirable practice.

The fourth element is to *resolve problems* by implementing some type of corrective action. A variety of remedial activities are possible. For instance, physicians may be contacted directly, educational programs may be put in place, or formulary and prior authorization restrictions may be imposed.

The final step is to *evaluate the DUR program* again after attempts have been made to correct problems. This is done by comparing actual use to the standards of appropriate therapy to see if the situation has changed. Have problems been corrected? Has quality improved? In other words, is drug utilization better now than it was before the DUR, based on the criteria that define quality?

Drug Focus

A DUR program should have one of three areas of focus: (1) profiles of physician prescribers; (2) a particular drug or class of drugs; or

(3) an individual patient's prescription drug use.

Prescriber profiles are retrospective, or after the fact, in nature, in that they use already paid claims as a database. Drug therapy has been started and possibly completed by the time the analysis is undertaken.

Potential indicators include: percent of patients receiving one or more drugs; prescriptions per visit; percent of prescriptions for generic products; and (for a particular medication) percent of prescriptions of a designated class.

This profiling process can serve several purposes. First, it gives a statistical picture of drug use for an entire patient population and any drug utilization problems that might be present. Over time, trends in drug use can be analyzed based on this data. Second, a physician's own prescribing patterns can be identified, analyzed and compared with his or her peers.

Physician profiling identifies doctors who consistently prescribe, for example, needlessly expensive medication when there are more economical alternatives, doctors who use a class of drugs for inappropriate indications, or ones who are frequently noncompliant with the formulary. Physician profiling can answer questions like: Is a physician using the drug of choice more or less frequently than his or her colleagues? Is a physician using expensive brand-name products rather than less expensive generics more or less frequently than his or her peers? The relatively new science of detecting and preventing inappropriate prescribing, either on a patient population or physician-by-physician basis, is called *pharmacoepidemiology*.[19]

Results of analyses comparing physicians to each other can serve as the basis for changes such as developing prescriber education programs, modifying benefit design and developing provider incentives to prescribe generics rather than brand-name drugs.

Three educational approaches are common.[20] The first and most intense is face-to-face education with a clinical pharmacist. Called *counterdetailing*, the strategy uses pharmacists specially trained not only in the pharmacology of classes of drugs but in educational techniques shown to be effective in changing physician behavior. (The practice is similar to detailing, explained in Chapter 4, where pharmaceutical company sales representatives call on doctors to try to persuade them to prescribe a particular drug.)

The second approach uses the mail and telephone. Here the doctor is sent by mail a profile of his or her own prescribing patterns, as well as relevant educational material. The doctor then receives a follow-up phone call from a clinical pharmacist or educator to discuss the materials and profile.

The third and least intensive approach uses the mail only, without the followup phone contact. Data suggest these educational methods are very effective and can yield a minimum return on the invested educational dollar of four to one.[21]

If these efforts don't result in changes in prescribing, physicians who continue to be noncompliant might receive written advisories or be subject to penalties, such as not being able to receive risk pool bonuses.

A second focus of DUR is a *particular drug or drug class*. The intent is to assess current practices and trends with the goal of detecting problems that might diminish the quality or cost-effectiveness of care. This type of review is also often retrospective and identifies problems that have already occurred.

Certain drugs tend to be especially good candidates for this kind of DUR. These drugs are usually:[22]

- Expensive
- Frequently prescribed
- Known or suspected to cause serious adverse reactions or otherwise be associated with significant health risks
- Used in patients at high risk for adverse drug reactions
- Potentially toxic or the source of discomfort at therapeutic doses (which leads to noncompliance or a change in therapy)
- Most effective when used in a specific manner, such as with certain other drugs or nondrug therapies.

The third possible DUR focus concerns *the therapies of individual patients*, which can be reviewed prospectively, concurrently or retrospectively.

Timing

A *prospective DUR program* involves review before a medication is dispensed to a patient. This type of review usually takes place in the pharmacy but, ideally, it would occur in the physician's office, though at this point relatively few doctors' offices are equipped with computer technology this advanced. This is due to a lack of protocols and communication standards to allow doctors access to an individual patient's claims database. Once this technology is widely available, the advancement of drug utilization review in general should be dramatic.

According to OBRA '90, the elements listed below should be screened *before* dispensing prescriptions (*prospectively*) to Medicaid recipients. However, they are equally valid criteria for general pharmacy practice. Elements to be checked include:[23]

- Therapeutic duplication
- Drug-disease contraindications
- Drug-drug interactions, including serious interactions with non-prescription products
- Incorrect drug dose or duration of therapy
- Drug-allergy interactions
- Clinical abuse or misuse.

Some pharmacies use only an in-house DUR system with customers presenting prescriptions to be filled. An increasing number, though, are also connected by a computerized point-of-sale (POS) system to the pharmacy benefits manager. The automated program screens prescriptions for potential problems like those above and sends a warning, or "stop," message, when necessary, to the pharmacist. These computerized messages are called *edits*. This real-time, online DUR provides pharmacists with access to far more complete patient and drug use data than they have on their own. Sophisticated systems identify potential adverse reactions, toxicities and contraindications so that pharmacists can adjust drug therapy before a medication that might be inappropriate or harmful is actually dispensed.

There are several advantages to PBMs of a POS prospective DUR system versus stand-alone, individual pharmacy systems. First, POS capabilities save money for the payer when patients can be switched (at the appropriate time) from a costly medication for an acute health problem to a less expensive maintenance medication. These cost savings on a per patient basis may not seem large, but when multiplied by thousands of plan members, the savings can be substantial over time. Second, pharmacy benefits managers can be certain with a POS drug utilization review that all prescriptions are uniformly screened, regardless of which pharmacy patients patronize. Although pharmacies may be able to ignore or decline DUR messages when they appear on the computer screen, the PBM's contract with pharmacies can be written to encourage or even require that POS messages be received and reviewed. Third, POS DUR screening can encompass the entire drug history of a particular patient. Individual pharmacies typically only have access to information on prescriptions filled there and have no way of knowing what other medications have been dispensed by other pharmacies.

Concurrent drug review of individual patient therapies can occur in two different ways. A pharmacist can review a patient's drug regimen on a periodic basis, as is required for Medicare and Medicaid patients in long-term care facilities (discussed in more detail later in this chapter). A second form of concurrent review is performed by some PBMs that screen prescriptions based on processed claim forms. If a problem is detected, the physician is alerted. According to one PBM, currently one in 11 prescriptions is questioned under concurrent review.[24]

*Retrospective review–or patient profiling–*is the third type of review of individual patient therapies. The drawback to retrospective review, of course, is that the process cannot prevent problems that have already occurred. However, one advantage is that the most complete information is available for review once the entire dispensing process is complete.

In this case, patients' prescription histories, based on their claims, are checked against criteria similar to those mentioned above in concurrent and prospective reviews. In addition, other criteria such as total number or total dollar value of prescriptions may be used. The system flags patients who are at high risk for a potential drug-related problem, and their cases are reviewed by a committee of pharmacists and physicians. Depending on how the DUR system is set up, the information available to the review committee can range from detailed medical records to claims histories. If the problem is serious, the pharmacies and physicians involved in the patient's care are contacted and therapeutic changes are recommended.

Drug Regimen Review (DRR)

As we noted near the beginning of this chapter, the intent of drug regimen review (DRR) is to identify inappropriate or potentially harmful drug therapy. It's been used in hospitals and long-term care facilities since at least the 1960s, mandated by state and federal regulations. In 1987, outcomes-oriented regulations were instituted under the Omnibus Budget Reconciliation Act (OBRA '87) covering issues related to drug therapy such as monitoring, patient rights, outcomes management and quality of life.[25]

Long-term care pharmacists are usually described as provider pharmacists, consultant pharmacists or both. Provider pharmacists focus on the drug delivery and distribution system, including labeling, packaging, maintenance of medication profiles, record and audit systems, and drug distribution. Consultant pharmacists emphasize drug use and drug use policies, with the key activity being drug regimen review that optimizes desired therapeutic outcomes.[26] Today, many long-term care pharmacists handle both functions.

Federal regulations state that patient charts in long-term care facilities must be reviewed on a monthly basis. Irregularities must be documented, and recommendations must be suggested to the medical and nursing staff. A typical DRR might provide the following information about an individual patient's drug therapy:[27]

- ◑ The use of a medication without an appropriate diagnosis
- ◑ The use of an inappropriate medication dosage
- ◑ Concurrent use of potentially interactive medications
- ◑ The use of duplicate therapy
- ◑ Continued use of a medication that's no longer necessary
- ◑ The presence of a medication-related adverse reaction.

The Downside of Drug Utilization Review

It's important for payers to understand the shortcomings and dangers of DUR. Though its purpose should be to determine and maintain appropriate drug use, too often it's done mainly to control costs. In fact, DUR is sometimes said to stand for "drug use restriction" and DUE for "drug use elimination." It should be designed and used to monitor the appropriateness of drug use and provide employers with feedback regarding utilization levels and trends. Payers that implement DUR programs should make sure they achieve these goals rather than focusing on cutting costs and identifying errant physician outliers.

> *DUR should focus primarily on monitoring the appropriateness of drug use rather than controlling costs.*

Although DUR is extremely important, it's not an easy, quick process to implement or maintain. There are a number of barriers to developing and sustaining an effective DUR program:[28]

- ◑ *Incomplete and inaccessible drug utilization data.* Some data may be available but inaccurate or difficult to access. Large quantities of paper reports can also be unwieldy.
- ◑ *Clearly defined drug utilization standards.* Plans may not identify or clarify what acceptable or ideal utilization patterns are, or these may not be accepted and followed by prescribers.
- ◑ *Adequate clinical pharmacy resources.* In some plans, there are not enough clinical pharmacists to communicate adequately with prescribers when DUR detects problems. There may be, for instance, as many as 1,000 prescribers for every clinical pharmacist.
- ◑ *Lack of support for DUR activities by plans and/or payers.* Payers may be unwilling to fund comprehensive DUR programs until significant effects are noted.
- ◑ *Lack of ability to merge pharmacy and medical databases.* Most

plans don't have the technological ability to link pharmacy and medical databases in order to properly evaluate medical outcomes associated with drugs.

Utilization Reports

Pharmacy benefits managers submit various types of reports to their clients containing some of the information derived from the DURs they manage. How often these reports are required varies with individual contracts. Report elements typically deal with three major issues:

1. Overall use and cost
2. Use and cost adjusted for membership
3. Use and cost by drug class and drug product related to use by the entire plan membership.

Overall Use and Cost

Total number of prescriptions = number of prescription claims paid during reporting period.

Total cost of prescriptions = total dollars spent for prescriptions during reporting period, including amount paid through patient cost-sharing.

Cost per prescription = total cost of prescriptions divided by total number of prescriptions.

Total benefit payments = total amount paid by the payer for prescriptions (via the PBM), excluding member cost-sharing amounts. This total may include the PBM's administrative charges.

Benefit payment per prescription = total amount paid by the plan divided by total number of prescriptions.

"Popular" drugs = number of prescriptions and total dollars spent for each of the drugs with the highest expenditures or highest number of prescriptions (usually limited to top ten to 50 drugs).

Use and Cost Adjusted for Membership

Member-months = number of months each member was enrolled in the plan during the reporting period.

Number of recipients = number of members receiving at least one prescription during the reporting period. Also expressed as percent of members, indicating proportion of members using the benefit.

Prescriptions per member-months = total number of prescriptions divided by number of member-months during reporting period.

Prescriptions per recipient = total number of prescriptions divided by number of prescription recipients during reporting period.

Use by Drug Type or Class

Use by drug product and therapeutic class = number of prescriptions and dollars spent for each drug and for each therapeutic class during reporting period. Also expressed as percent of total prescriptions or dollars.

Use of generic products = number of prescriptions filled with generic products. Also expressed as percent of total prescriptions.

Prescriber Profiles

In addition, *prescriber profiles* may be produced as described earlier. These provide data on individual prescribing physicians, which may be compared to data from their peers. *Patient profiles*, which provide data on specific patients, can also be generated. These reports are useful in DUR and provider education programs. Example report elements include:

- ◗ *Total prescriptions*: expressed as number of prescriptions and their dollar value
- ◗ *Cost per prescription*
- ◗ *Generic prescriptions*: expressed as percent of total prescriptions
- ◗ *Prescriptions for specified products* (usually less effective, riskier, or more expensive than alternatives): number of prescriptions, also expressed as percent of total prescriptions for a drug class.

Patient Profiles (Claims Listings)

Generally, a patient profile is a listing of all that patient's prescriptions, including data available from the claim form.

For each prescription during the specified time period, the listing would include:

- ◗ Pharmacy
- ◗ Prescriber
- ◗ Drug, strength and dosage form
- ◗ Quantity and days' supply
- ◗ Whether new or refill
- ◗ Date filled
- ◗ Cost data.

The key is deciding which patient profiles or listings should be generated. These may be patients who have:

- ◗ Specific diseases or diagnoses

○ A high number of prescriptions (greater than a specified number)
○ High drug cost (cost of prescriptions greater than a specified amount)
○ Duplicate therapy (more than one drug from a therapeutic class)
○ Received a specified drug or drug class (drugs known to be risky or costly).

Questions to Ask About Drug Utilization Review (DUR)

1. What type of drug utilization review(s) does the PBM conduct (DUR, DRR, DUE, etc.)?

2. Does the PBM have a *prospective* DUR program? Does it use a point-of-sale (POS) system? What are its capabilities? What percent of prescriptions receive a warning message? What percent of messages result in a pharmacist action?

3. Does the PBM have a *concurrent* DUR system? What percent of prescriptions result in an action? What percent of actions result in a change in therapy?

4. Does the PBM have a *retrospective* DUR system? Describe how it works. Is it focused on (1) prescribers? (2) patients? and/or (3) drugs or drug classes? What is the rationale behind these choices?

5. Is there a formal process to establish or revise quality standards or criteria for evaluating drug use? Who is responsible for making decisions about quality?

6. Are prescriber and/or patient profiles available? What criteria are used in selecting profiles for review?

7. After reports or profiles are generated, is there a specific process to identify problems and take corrective action? Who is responsible for this function?

8. What utilization reports are generated by the PBM to monitor trends and manage drug use and expenditures? When are these produced? In what form? Are they clear and understandable?

9. What education programs or other corrective actions have resulted from DUR during the past _____ months? What has been their outcome?

Endnotes

1. "Integrating a Pharmacy Benefits Program Into a Managed Healthcare Plan" (Chicago: American Association of Preferred Provider Organizations, 1991), 7.
2. Ibid.

3. "The Expanding Role of PBMs," *Business & Health Special Report: Pharmacy Benefits Management: The Next Generation*, 1995, 7.

4. J. R. Lang, "Drug Utilization Review and the New Managed Care Pharmacy," *Medical Interface*, February 1993, 49.

5. "Drug Utilization: The Ultimate Strategy," *Business & Health Special Report: Managed Care Comes to Prescription Drug Benefits*, 1991, 20.

6. Ibid., 21.

7. Ibid.

8. "Study Finds Adverse Drug Events Cost More Than Drugs Themselves," *Pharmacy Practice News*, January 1995, 1.

9. Ibid.

10. Ibid., 2.

11. "Opportunities Presented by Drug Utilization Review," *Medical Interface*, February 1993, 44.

12. B. Briesacher and J. DuChane, "Drug Utilization Review in the Managed Care Environment," *Medical Interface*, March 1995, 72.

13. Marion Merrell Dow, *Managed Care Digest*/HMO Edition, 1994, 37.

14. Ibid., 36.

15. Ibid., 37.

16. *Principles of Drug Use Review (DUR)* (Washington, DC: American Medical Association, American Pharmaceutical Association, and Pharmaceutical Manufacturers Association, 1991).

17. G. F. Farr, "Clinical Applications and Drug Use Review," in B. R. Canaday, ed., *OBRA '90: A Practical Guide to Effecting Pharmaceutical Care* (American Pharmaceutical Association, 1994).

18. "ASHP Guidelines on the Pharmacist's Role in Drug Use Evaluation," *American Journal of Hospital Pharmacy* 45 (1988): 385-386.

19. Lang, "Drug Utilization Review and the New Managed Care Pharmacy," 52.

20. Ibid.

21. Ibid.

22. Ibid.

23. W. L. Fitzgerald, "Legal Control of Pharmacy Services," in B. R. Canaday, ed., *OBRA '90: A Practical Guide to Effecting Pharmacy Care* (American Pharmaceutical Association, 1994).

24. "The Expanding Role of PBMs," 8.

25. B. M. Schechter and P. P. Gerbino, "The Role of the Pharmacist in Long-Term Care," *Medical Interface*, April 1992, 54.

26. Ibid., 56.

27. "The Role of the Pharmacist in Long-Term Care," 59.

28. R. P. Navarro, "DUR Applications in Managed Care," *Medical Interface*, March 1995, 67-68.

Many experts believe that managed care, still a very young industry, has already evolved to the point where it has entered a "next generation" status. Beginning with an initial focus on cost control, then moving to an emphasis on quality and accessibility, American health care has made dramatic strides in the last ten to 15 years under the sizable umbrella of the managed care philosophy. All these stepping stones, however, while critically important, had little to do with the direct management of the care of patients with specific diseases. The currently blossoming new generation of managed care is characterized, therefore, by several important core concepts that address the individual patient's total health care picture from start to finish.

Chapter 6...

Beyond Prescription Benefits Management:
The Systems Approach to Patient and Pharmaceutical Care

The Systems Approach

At first, managed care perpetuated the traditional component-based health care system, characterized by a fragmented approach that treated each incidence of illness separately. The component model attempted to contain costs, but because it was not an integrated system, it did little to influence the tremendous long-term expense of chronic illnesses.

The component model of health care management fails to adequately control health care costs for a number of reasons:[1]

- ◑ It does not recognize that health care components are interrelated.
- ◑ All diseases are treated the same, even though different diseases have different cost structures and respond differently to prevention and treatment.

◑ In many cases, the component model favors treatment over prevention.

◑ It results in an uncoordinated delivery system without continuity of care.

◑ It often pays for the most expensive services in the most expensive setting.

◑ It lacks incentives for providers to understand and treat the entire disease process.

◑ It weakens, rather than strengthens, the physician-patient relationship.

◑ It sometimes encourages an adversarial relationship between health care managers and physicians.

Managed care is moving from a component approach to an integrated systems model.

Managed care is now moving toward an integrated systems model of health care delivery and financing. Unlike the component approach, the systems model views health care (from a population standpoint as well as on a patient-by-patient basis) on a continuum that stretches from prevention through screening, diagnosis, treatment, compliance, after care and outcomes studies.

This new model features an integration of resources unprecedented in the history of American health care. The goal of what are being called *integrated health management delivery systems (IHMDS)* is to "manage and measure the behavior of providers and patients with the outcome objective of achieving optimum patient wellness and disease prevention and treatment. [This is accomplished] through the most appropriate use of cost-effective products and services provided by a comprehensive managed health care delivery infrastructure."[2]

Data analysis and the application of research dealing with the outcome of certain treatments are important aspects of the systems approach. The new focus of this "big picture" model is disease management, but many say it's more accurately called *health* management to acknowledge the emphasis on wellness and the involvement of the entire spectrum of health care professionals, products and services. In contrast to the traditional focus on treating and/or curing disease once it has occurred, the systems/ health management approach emphasizes disease prevention and lifestyle issues such as stress reduction, fitness, smoking cessation and family planning.

Pharmacy is taking a leadership role in the new generation of managed care.

Pharmacy, not surprisingly, is taking a leadership role in this new generation of managed care. One reason is that pharmacy claims data provide perhaps the most complete and "truthful" record of treatment interventions. However, pharmacy claims show only one piece of the puzzle and should not be looked at in isolation. Many PBMs are promoting this central role for the pharmaceutical industry (particularly practicing pharmacists) because of their ability to collect, organize and provide drug utilization data as a "snapshot" of all sorts of disease treatment.

Pharmaceutical Care

In addition, there is a growing awareness of the pharmacist's ability to provide services that go far beyond pill dispensing in the confines of the pharmacy and into any health care setting that involves decisions about the use of medication. This new area, called *pharmaceutical care*, addresses the need for and the capability of pharmacists to provide optimal drug therapy that includes a comprehensive range of services to improve the overall quality of patients' lives and health. The optimal use of drugs, including cognitive services, produces therapeutic benefits to patients and financial benefits to payers.

It's now understood that pharmacy benefits actually have two components: (1) the dispensing of pharmaceutical *products* and (2) pharmaceutical *services*. In and of itself, a drug does not offer maximum potential benefits.[3] Instead, it's the *optimal use* of the drug that produces therapeutic benefits to patients and financial benefits to payers. Health plan design should actively encourage the utilization of pharmacists as experts in pharmaceutical science who act as advisers to both prescribers and patients. Few people realize how little training, comparatively speaking, physicians have in pharmacology and how *much* training and expertise pharmacists have. Pharmacists can and should take a consultant's role in advising patients and prescribers in both the positive aspects of drug therapy (such as monitoring drug use, coordinating prescriptions and optimizing drug therapy over the course of time) and the negative aspects, like preventing drug misuse, curbing inappropriate prescribing, and addressing/correcting patient and provider noncompliance.

These areas are becoming known as *cognitive,* or *professional, services,* which include such activities as pharmacists providing drug information and patient counseling about prescriptions and overall drug therapy; interventions with prescribers that influence the cost and efficacy of treatment; the development of quality improvement programs; the prevention, monitoring and reporting of adverse drug reactions; the documentation of pharmaceutical care in patient medical records; and a lengthening list of additional pharmacist-provided services that contribute to the overall optimization of patient health and wellness. The advantageous consequence of all these activities is that they will help control costs and influence outcomes. When the mission is accomplished, proponents say, the triad of managed care objectives (quality, cost control and accessibility) will be realized.

A number of studies have demonstrated that pharmacists' professional services have improved patient outcomes, reduced the cost of drug therapy and improved physicians' prescribing practices.[4] In one study that surveyed patients, for example, 61% stated that counseling by their pharmacist reduced doctor office visits. Four other studies showed that patients took less medication when pharmacists consulted with their doctors about their drug regimens. A study of physicians' prescribing errors found that the additional cost of compensating pharmacists for discussing these errors with prescribers resulted in saving four times the cost of paying the pharmacists for consultation.[5]

In one study of Medicaid drug utilization review (DUR), researchers found that when prescribers of three medications that were often overused were encouraged to reconsider their prescribing, Medicaid drug expenses dropped at three times the cost of the DUR.

However, attempts to cut costs can backfire and make matters worse. A well-known example was a 1991 study of the New Hampshire Medicaid system reported in the *New England Journal of Medicine*.[6] In 1981, in an attempt to cut prescription drug costs in its Medicaid program, New Hampshire set a cap of three prescriptions per month per recipient. The move was projected to save $300,000 to $400,000 a year but instead produced adverse results all around. Although drug utilization fell by 35% during the cap period, admission rates to nursing homes were more than 50% greater than those in a control state, and hospitalizations increased drastically. Savings from lower drug costs were more than offset by the increased expense of institutionalization.

In a more recent study of the effects of the same prescription cap on Medicaid patients with schizophrenia, there were immediate reductions in the use of antipsychotic and antidepressant drugs, but the drug restrictions also caused far greater cost increases in the use of emergency mental health services.[7]

Practice Guidelines

One important aspect of how this systems focus is influencing the prescribing behavior of physicians is the standardization, for the first time, of treatment guidelines that are enforced through managed care strategies.

Practice guidelines (also known as *practice policies, treatment protocols* and *critical pathways*) are defined as recommendations issued in advance of the delivery of health care services to influence decisions about treatment interventions. According to the Institute of Medicine (IOM), clinical practice guidelines are "systematically developed statements to assist practitioner and patient decisions about appropriate health care for specific clinical circumstances." Because guidelines summarize prevailing medical knowledge and base recommendations on currently accepted diagnostic, therapeutic and medical management protocols for specific conditions, practice guidelines are like a road map, or even a step-by-step set of directions, that help doctors make more informed decisions about treatment.[8]

> *Standardized treatment guidelines can influence the prescribing behavior of physicians.*

Now that it's recognized that many patients with similar medical characteristics can be treated similarly, practice guidelines use data from large groups of patients to guide treatment decisions made about individual patients.

Practice guidelines are developed by numerous groups, including health care associations, medical specialty societies, managed care organizations (MCOs), research centers and hospitals. Practice policies for various medical conditions have also been developed by committees of experts (for example, the National Cholesterol Education Project) and by the federal government's Agency for Health Care Policy and Research (AHCPR). These "official" guidelines often serve as prototypes for the practice policies developed by "front line" organizations such as PBMs, hospitals and HMOs. Practice guidelines are often established by a health plan's pharmacy and therapeutics (P&T) committee or a similar evaluative group. (The P&T committee is discussed in Chapter 4 on Formularies.) In developing practice policies, the committee uses published research, internal data from drug use reviews and other data collection projects, expert opinions and input from various clinicians. In addition, the preferences of patients (or potential future patients) may also be considered.

Already, thousands of guidelines have been published on almost every medical condition. The American Medical Association's (AMA) *Directory of Practice Parameters*, for instance, lists 1,600 guidelines.[9] Practice guidelines can take a variety of forms: pages of text, step-by-step plans, or visual aids such as flowcharts or decision trees.[10]

According to the Marion Merrell Dow, *Managed Care Digest*/Medical Group Practice Edition, 1994, 31% of medical groups had formal practice guidelines or standards in 1993, with 60% of these groups saying their standards applied to primary care. Over two-thirds of the groups without practice policies in place planned to implement them during the next two years.

Ninety-six percent of groups with formal protocols were developed internally by the group practice. The largest medical groups, with more than 100 physicians, were the ones most likely to have developed practice policies and standards of care (64%), compared with just 28% of the smallest groups.[11]

As with formularies, practice guidelines relative to pharmaceuticals are intended to influence the cost and quality of medical care and drug therapy. However, pharmacy practice guidelines are more specific than formularies. Rather than simply listing recommended drug products, guidelines specify: (1) if, when and how a drug or other medical service should be used, or (2) the services that should be provided to patients with a particular condition.

> *Like formularies, pharmaceutical practice guidelines are intended to influence the cost and quality of medical care and drug therapy.*

Practice Policies in Pharmacy Benefits Management

Three factors underlie the increasing prevalence and importance of practice policies in pharmacy benefits management. One is the realization that practice policies are necessary to achieve efficiency in drug therapy (that is, obtaining the greatest improvement in health status at a given level of expenditure). Cost-efficiency cannot be achieved simply through price discounts from drug manufacturers. Pharmacy expenditures are a function of which products are used, their frequency of use and their per unit price. As mentioned earlier, financial decisions should not be based on pharmacy claims alone, as they show only part of the picture. Practice guidelines go beyond price guidelines and specifically address *which* products should be used and *how* they should be utilized in order to *maximize clinical* as well as economic efficiency.

The second factor, which is related to the first, is that the quality of patient care can be directly and positively affected by practice policies. Medical decision making is more complex today than ever before. Making rational treatment decisions involves the following steps: (1) The problem is defined; (2) alternative courses of action are identified; (3) the outcomes (both positive and negative) of each alternative are specified, along with the probability of their occurrence; (4) preferences among the various outcomes are determined; and (5) the best alternative is selected, in the judgment of the decision maker.

Because of the vast array of options available in modern medicine, totally rational decision making according to the above steps is extremely difficult, if not impossible. Medical decision making is subjective, to some extent, and characterized by uncertainty because there is so little published research about what is effective and what isn't. Due to this subjectivity, uncertainty and lack of data, practice guidelines are increasingly important because so many treatment decisions are simply too complicated today to be made on a one-by-one basis.

The third reason practice guidelines are becoming so important and prevalent in pharmacy benefits management is the recognition that all medical services—including drug therapy—are means to an end: improved health status for patients. Medical services can be used in a variety of combinations, and using one service can sometimes diminish the need for another kind of service. In other cases, a service may be more effective if used in combination with another one.

> **Three Types of Practice Policies**
> ◑ *Prescribing criteria*
> ◑ *Treatment guidelines*
> ◑ *Disease state management (DSM)*

From this perspective, the primary issue is not the quality or cost of the pharmacy benefit alone, although these are still significant. The larger issue is treating and even preventing diseases and the overall cost and quality by which this is accomplished, according to the systems approach described earlier.

Types of Practice Policies

There are three types of practice policies. The first is *prescribing criteria*, which focus on the appropriate use of a particular drug or drug class. The specific criteria involved indicate for whom and how that drug or drug class should be prescribed. Generally, prescribing criteria are most beneficial when used with drugs that are: (1) unusually potent or high risk, (2) expensive and/or (3) effective in well-defined but limited cases.

Prescribing criteria play a central role in prospective drug utilization review (DUR) because the PBM can potentially learn more about a particular drug therapy situation through claims forms than with a medical diagnosis alone. Prior authorization (described in Chapter 4) is also used in conjunction with prescribing criteria, as the system may require approval from the pharmacy benefits manager before a prescription is dispensed as a covered service.

The second type of practice policies is *treatment guidelines* which, in contrast to prescribing criteria, focus on a disease or a set of patients instead of a drug or drug class. These guidelines describe how drug therapy should be used for this disease or group of patients. Treatment guidelines indicate drugs of choice (first-line therapies) for a disease and can also include steps to be taken if the first choice fails.

The third type of practice policies involves *disease state management (DSM)*, a comprehensive approach to treating chronic or high-cost illnesses. DSM will be covered in detail later in this chapter.

The Process of Developing Practice Policies

Practice policies fall into two general categories: *implicit* and *explicit*. *Implicit policies* are qualitative guidelines whose development is based on the opinions of experts. *Explicit policies*, in contrast, are essentially quantitative and involve systemic analysis and hard data. While explicit practice policies are more difficult to develop, they also tend to be more influential in changing physicians' practice patterns. In general, pharmacy practice policies are evolving from a state of being largely implicit, or subjective, to being explicit, that is, based on fact and research data.

> *Practice guidelines fall into two categories: implicit (based on opinion) and explicit (based on fact).*

There are *four steps involved in developing an explicit practice policy.*[12] These incorporate quantitative evidence, preferences and clinical judgment. The *first step* involves estimating the positive and negative outcomes of an intervention, whether that is a drug, service or medical procedure. This analytical process calls for an evaluation and synthesis of the available research evidence and data. It also involves clinical judgment or expertise, because quantitative evidence can never be considered a finite entity. This scrutiny provides a summary of benefits and risks.

The *second step* is to compare these benefits and risks. Deciding whether the benefits outweigh the risks is largely a matter of the personal judgment of a skilled clinician or group of practitioners.

The *third step* may also involve personal judgment. If the benefits have been determined to exceed the risks, the costs of the intervention are estimated, and these costs are compared to the net benefit (benefit minus risk). This step results in the net value to patients (*net value* is the difference between net benefit and cost).

If resources are unlimited (rarely the case anymore, thanks to the mandates of managed care, not to mention reality), any drug, service or procedural intervention with a positive net value can be provided. However, when resources *are* limited, a *fourth step* is necessary. With limited resources, the net benefit and cost of the intervention must be compared to the net benefit and cost of other interventions. This allows priorities to be set that yield the greatest benefit possible based on the available resources. When resources are very limited, the use of a given intervention may not be justifiable at all, even when its benefit exceeds its cost. (See the section on pharmacoeconomics later in this chapter for more detailed information on measuring long-term benefit and cost.)

Practice policies work especially well in staff model HMOs, because their concentrated and integrated nature can influence and guide the treatment decisions made by in-house physicians. One PPO is developing its own computerized question and answer format to guide physicians through the process of making a diagnosis, selecting the appropriate treatment and choosing the most effective and economical drug for that particular patient. The program will eventually be sold to other health care entities.[13]

Developing practice guidelines, especially explicit ones, is not a simple, straightforward process. As with formularies, the credibility of a particular practice policy is affected not only by its scientific merit but by the reputation of its developers and the rationale behind their recommendations.

Disease State Management (DSM)

Disease state management (DSM) (also called *disease management* and *disease-based management*) is arguably the most significant and widespread new trend in managed care. DSM is at the heart of the next generation of managed care because it takes the concept of improving cost, quality and access one step further by focusing on chronic, costly medical conditions that require long-term treatment. Chronic diseases are typically targeted because that's where most health care dollars are spent, and it's also the area where prevention strategies can have the greatest effect. Through a combination of pharmaceutical care, practice guidelines, data management, and patient and provider interventions, DSM aims to control the cost of certain diseases by utilizing the most effective treatment modalities as early in a patient's "disease state" as possible. The goal of disease state management is to achieve a successful outcome in a cost-effective manner.

DSM-appropriate diseases include diabetes (which accounts for 13% of a health plan's costs while afflicting just 3% of its members) and asthma (which cost the United States $3.6 billion in 1990 in medical costs and $2.6 billion in indirect costs, such as time lost from work). Depression and hypertension also respond well to DSM.[14]

DSM assumes that there are numerous inefficiencies in every health care delivery system. By pinpointing these problems and finding innovative, proactive ways to resolve them, the DSM approach attempts to permit providers to deliver value at *all* points in the continuum, all the way from prevention through outcomes research.

> *Disease state management controls the cost of certain diseases by utilizing the most effective treatment modalities as early in a patient's "disease state" as possible.*

DSM exemplifies the systems (versus component) approach to comprehensive health care described at the beginning of this chapter. Consider the example of an insulin-dependent diabetic patient who must be taken to a hospital emergency room during a medical crisis. No matter how good that hospital's care is, it won't be cost-effective or efficient from either the patient or payer viewpoint because it's being implemented as a fairly isolated component of care. The systems approach, in contrast, could have prevented the attack entirely through patient education and compliance motivation. This would cost far less than emergency room treatment and a possible hospital stay. Critics of the traditional component approach also note that health care providers are not required to take any responsibility for the occurrence and consequences of acute episodes, which, paradoxically, they are then financially rewarded for treating.[15]

Disease state management is really a specialized kind of proactive case management[16] in that it's a process where there is active intervention in the prevention, diagnosis and management of targeted diseases. A treatment algorithm is created that includes practice policies and standards of care that providers, case managers, patients and payers are encouraged (or required, in some cases) to follow. This approach empowers patients, primary care providers and specialists through education and targeted incentives to understand and work toward positive clinical and economic outcomes for a particular disease. At the end of the spectrum, outcomes can be tracked and data collected in an organized, standardized fashion that can be used in continuously improving the system's quality and effectiveness.

The disease state management concept is currently exciting to different participants in health care for different reasons. Employers hope it's a way to keep employees healthier and on the job, increase their satisfaction with their benefits and reduce health care costs. Drug companies see it as a potentially powerful way for them to enhance their image and increase product sales and market share. Managed health care organizations view DSM in terms of standardizing treatment protocols for common disorders and assuring appropriate utilization and quality care for patients.

DSM programs are proliferating rapidly, sponsored by pharmaceutical companies, PBM firms, health plans and proprietary interests. In some cases, the DSM program is essentially product based in that it's linked to the product line of a particular manufacturer. Others are therapeutic based in terms of having a more objective focus without ties to particular drug products or drug companies.

Pharmaceutical companies have taken an especially strong role in the development of DSM programs. Although they are not directly involved in patient care, manufacturers can be helpful at the front end of DSM by identifying the total cost of an illness when untreated; modeling both the natural history of a disease and the costs of treatment; conducting outcomes research to determine the appropriate use and effectiveness of a therapy; creating patient and provider education and compliance programs; and developing and possibly funding model DSM programs and building partnerships with MCOs.[17]

One expert estimates that 50% of total health care costs could be saved through the use of disease management systems.[18] However, some industry observers are skeptical about their effectiveness, either because they question the real or

> *One expert estimates that 50% of total health care costs could be saved through the use of disease state management.*

perceived conflict of interest associated with ties to pharmaceutical manufacturers or because so few studies of DSM cost-effectiveness have been completed. The lack of hard data means that purchasers of DSM programs find it difficult, if not impossible, to determine the true ability of such programs to enhance treatment quality and save money. To complicate matters, it's entirely possible that a DSM program could cost more initially but save money in the long run, much like a drug that costs more than others but results in significant overall savings down the line.

Obstacles to Implementing
a Disease State Management Program

For a number of reasons, disease state management programs can be difficult to develop and sustain successfully. One expert lists these potential obstacles:[19]

⬤ Fragmentation of care delivery systems

⬤ Incentives and inconsistencies in health care financing

⬤ Training and experience of providers

⬤ The component management orientation of purchaser and provider

⬤ Deficiencies in information systems and databases

⬤ Lack of useful and credible outcomes data

⬤ Weak or unenforced formularies and/or practice guidelines

⬤ Distrust between manufacturers (if they're involved) and providers.

However, the uncertainty and current lack of research data don't appear to be deterring most health plans from either implementing their own or purchasing DSM programs. According to a recent study of 62 managed care organizations by the Zitter Group in San Francisco, more than half were considering, developing or had already implemented disease state management programs.

> *According to a recent study, more than half of 62 MCOs polled were in the process of implementing a DSM program.*

One expert believes DSM will gain momentum as:[20]

⬤ Health system integration accelerates, offering providers broader control over entire diseases.

⬤ Information systems and databases evolve, enhancing data quality and facilitating tracking across care settings.

⬤ Capitation becomes more prevalent, providing incentives to minimize total illness costs (versus component-based costs).

⬤ Outcomes studies proliferate, offering insight into the effectiveness of treatment alternatives.

⬤ Practice guidelines are implemented, suggesting improved therapeutic strategies.

⬤ Utilization review and formulary enforcement become more sophisticated, increasing standardization of care.

⬤ Providers become more experienced in outcomes measurement and quality improvement, enabling these tools to be incorporated into the disease management process.

⬤ Manufacturers and MCOs learn to share risk, building a foundation for disease management partnerships.

Experts all caution that DSM is a process, not an objective or end-point. For many payers, the maximum return on their investment may not be realized for up to ten years. It's likely that some won't be willing to wait that long.

Outcomes Research: The Basis for Change

Put simply, *outcomes* can be defined as analyzing and measuring what happens to patients as a result of their treatment. At one time in the past, *outcomes* referred more narrowly to mortality (incidence of death), but the concept has expanded to include broader issues such as lives saved, hospitalizations averted or shortened, and patient satisfaction with care and quality of life.

Outcomes research is a major concept in health care today for good reason. It's a central element in the disease state management continuum as well as being a feature that payers are demanding with increasing frequency. Combined with cost information, outcomes data is an important decision making tool for payers. Purchasers are concerned not simply with cost, but with what they're getting for their health care dollar.

Outcomes studies, for example, might measure whether patients receive more benefit from drug therapy than from surgery. Or research might determine whether it's more beneficial to give antibiotics 12 hours, or two hours, before surgery to avoid postoperative infections.

The need for more research and universally meaningful data to use in outcomes research is very clear.

The evolution of outcomes research is being slowed by a scarcity of accurate and complete medical and claims data, and a sufficient number of years' worth of information upon which to base published results of outcomes studies. The need for more research and universally meaningful data is very clear. One outcomes expert estimates that between one-half and four-fifths of major medical treatments (even those that are effective) are not backed by solid scientific studies.[21] It's precisely this startling lack of comparative study that outcomes research seeks to remedy.

The federal government, for one, is aggressively pursuing outcomes research, having spent $200 million on patient outcomes studies in 1994.[22] However, in spite of all the talk, not everyone is actively embracing outcomes studies quite yet. *The 1994 Survey on Outcomes Management*, a recent study conducted by benefits consultants Foster Higgins on the prevalence of outcomes programs, showed that only 24% of health plans were "extremely active" or "very active" in outcomes research, and 32% said they were "not at all active." The inactive health plans cited lack of demand by employer groups as being responsible for their lack of activity, but 84% of the plans said that "greater employer interest in results" would cause them to expand their efforts.[23]

The development of electronic data interchange (EDI) networks promises to go a long way toward collecting and organizing encounter and pharmacy claims data to use in outcomes research. These EDIs provide electronic networks that may someday link every physician, hospital, laboratory, health care provider and pharmacy with every managed care plan and insurance carrier in the country—or even the world. This total integration would allow health plans to construct a complete picture of costs and utilization and sort their data by member, provider, diagnosis, procedure or drug.[24] Electronic data will also help P&T committees determine which drugs are the most effective and economical choices for inclusion on a plan's formulary.

Pharmacoeconomics

Pharmacoeconomics, one of the most powerful new weapons in the arsenal of outcomes research that is shaping health care decision making, is a specific type of research that is gaining momentum and prominence. Pharmacoeconomics is a decision making tool that uses mathematical formulas to compare and integrate costs and outcomes of drugs and other treatment options. It offers a number of new ways to compare drugs and make decisions that are both medically effective and cost conscious. Pharmacoeconomics data are being used increasingly in making hospital formulary decisions, developing clinical practice guidelines for drug use and identifying the overall cost impact of new pharmaceuticals.

The days when treatment decisions were left entirely to a physician's discretion are all but gone. With wide variations in clinical practice patterns, payers and even patients are beginning to demand quantitative data that demonstrate the superiority of one approach over another in terms of cost, quality of care and outcome. Many experts predict that before long, insurance companies will cover only those treatments that research has proven to be effective and efficient. In response to pressure from government, managed care organizations and consumers, researchers are currently creating vast databases of outcomes information in order to narrow practice variations, identify what works and what doesn't with similar patient groups, and determine the most cost-effective approach to treatment.

Pharmacoeconomics uses complicated mathematical formulas to measure long-term costs. Four models are commonly used:[25]

- ❍ *A cost-benefit analysis* weighs a drug's benefits (efficacy, safety, convenience) against its direct costs (purchasing, stocking, dispensing) and indirect costs (quality of life, lost workdays).
- ❍ *A cost-utility analysis* measures therapeutic outcome in quantitative and qualitative terms. For instance, a quantitative factor might be the cost per day of therapy multiplied by the average number of days that therapy is required. A qualitative factor might be the number of "quality adjusted" life years that a cancer or AIDS drug makes possible.
- ❍ *A cost-effectiveness analysis* compares similar agents and determines which drug achieves its therapeutic goal with the least cost. For example, if one product is 90% effective and another is 80% effective, there's a 10% difference. Dividing this difference into the cost difference produces a cost-effectiveness ration.
- ❍ *A cost-avoidance analysis* measures the costs of different drugs against future costs that they might prevent, such as costs for additional drugs, office visits, hospitalizations, surgery, long-term care and lost productivity.

Pharmacoeconomics is differentiated from older, less specific types of outcomes research because it expands the range of outcomes measurements to include not only standard clinical measures like response to treatment and mortality and morbidity, but nonclinical factors such as return to work, use of health care resources and quality of life. It gives both clinicians and researchers a more exact tool for quantifying costs, including direct medical costs (drugs, lab tests, hospitalizations and doctor office visits) and nonmedical resources such as time lost from work and the efforts of family caregivers.

Pharmacoeconomics is especially important in comparing cost and quality issues in the treatment of chronic, costly diseases such as cancer, AIDS and infectious diseases. The economic issues in these serious, long-term diseases are more intense than in other areas of health care because of opposing forces that are simultaneously driving up costs. These include the development, on one hand, of new, expensive drugs, the introduction of breakthrough biotechnology products, and the growth in dose-intensified treatment regimens, particularly in cancer treatments such as chemotherapy. On the other hand, forces such as reimbursement denials for off-label drug use and participation in clinical trials, as well as the rapid growth of managed care programs, are attempting to hold costs down. Even as these opposing forces battle over health care expenditures, pharmacoeconomics will provide a comparison of the costs and consequences of pharmaceutical products and services.

Pharmacoeconomic clinical trials differ from traditional clinical trials in several ways. Clinical trials limit studies to narrow, carefully controlled patient populations and focus on clinical outcomes such as endpoints and side effects. Pharmacoeconomic trials use broader populations more typical of actual patients and include clinical outcomes as part of a bigger picture. This approach looks at patient outcomes such as quality of life and economic outcomes such as cost-effectiveness, cost-minimization, cost-benefit analysis and cost-utility analysis. This broader, yet more specific focus provides payers with better data about the cost-benefit ratio of specific drugs.[26]

Drug companies are using the results of pharmacoeconomic clinical trials of their products to convince customers that their drugs are more cost-effective than the competition's. For instance, even when individual dosage costs are higher, if recovery times are shorter, the end result is lower overall therapeutic costs.

What's Ahead?

Outcomes studies and, especially, pharmacoeconomics research will play a huge part in future decisions about health care quality and cost control, including the use of drugs as an integral part of the patient care systems continuum. Price discounts are no longer sufficient to control costs through benefits management. The wave of the future is *therapy management*, an umbrella term that encompasses outcomes research, economic evaluation, treatment protocols, and provider and patient compliance. It involves the process of defining and implementing a certain regimen for the management of a particular disease, based on a specific diagnosis. This all occurs within the context of a systems–rather than a component–approach to lifelong health care that begins with aggressive efforts to prevent disease and encourage wellness. It ends, ideally, with the study of what medical treatments (including drugs) work with specific diseases and patient populations, what doesn't work, and what documented value both payers and patients are getting for the money they spend.

Questions to Ask About Practice Policies, Prescribing Criteria, DSM and Outcomes Research

1. What are your philosophies and practices regarding pharmaceutical care and pharmacists' cognitive services? What incentives do you offer pharmacists to perform these services? What reimbursement do you provide pharmacists for cognitive services?

2. Do you have a formal process to develop practice policies (criteria, guidelines and disease state management programs)? What is it? Who is responsible for developing and approving practice policies?

3. Are practice policies formally and periodically evaluated and revised? How and by whom?

4. What methods are used to disseminate and explain practice policies to providers?

5. What methods are used to encourage the adoption of practice policies?

6. Are prescribing criteria available? For what drugs?

7. Are treatment guidelines available? For what diseases?

8. Are DSM programs available? For what diseases? Describe them. What evidence do you have that they are effective?

9. What, if any, outcomes research do you conduct? What is it used for? Are any DSM programs linked to outcomes research?

10. Do you conduct or have access to pharmacoeconomic research data?

11. What data integration capabilities do you have?

Endnotes

1. Naughton Cohen, "Systems Management" (Washington, DC: Pharmaceutical Research and Manufacturers of America), 67.
2. R. Navarro, "Integrated Health Management Delivery System," *Medical Interface*, August 1994, 64-68.
3. *Achieving Value From Pharmacists' Services* (Washington, DC: American Pharmaceutical Association, 1994), 7.
4. Ibid., 23-24.
5. Ibid.
6. S. B. Soumerai et al., "Effects of Medicaid Drug Payment Limits on Admission to Hospitals and Nursing Homes," *New England Journal of Medicine* 325 (1991):1072-1077.
7. "Systems Management," 67.
8. *Managed Care Selling Edge*, July/August, 1994 (Boston: Total Learning Concepts, Inc., 1994), 8.
9. Ibid.

10. Ibid.

11. Marion Merrell Dow, *Managed Care Digest*/Medical Group Practice Edition, 1994, 29.

12. D. M. Eddy, "A Manual for Assessing Health Practices and Designing Practice Policies: The Explicit Approach" (Philadelphia: American College of Physicians, 1992).

13. C. Petersen, "Disease State Management: A New View of an Old Idea," *Managed Healthcare*, May 1995, 48.

14. "Disease Management: Continuous Health Care Improvement," *Business & Health*, April 1995, 67.

15. M. Zitter, "Pharmacy Practice," *Medical Interface*, August 1994, 72.

16. E. Zalta, H. Eichner and M. Henry, "Implications of Disease Management in the Future of Managed Care," *Medical Interface*, December 1994, 67.

17. Zitter, "Pharmacy Practice," 72.

18. Meeting Point, *Medical Interface*, January, 1995, 76.

19. Ibid., 70.

20. Zitter, "Pharmacy Practice," 75-76.

21. "Interest in Outcomes Research Is Growing Rapidly," *Business & Health Special Report: Putting Outcomes Research to Work*, 1992, 9.

22. Meeting Point, *Medical Interface*, 75.

23. R. Navarro, "The Risks and Rewards of Outcomes Management Systems," *Medical Interface*, November 1994, 82.

24. R. Navarro, "Changing the Marketing Message," *Medical Interface*, August 1993, 55.

25. "How Managed Health Care Organizations Control Pharmaceutical Costs," *The Managed Care Handbook*, 15-16.

26. *Managed Care Selling Edge*, 4.

I t's often said that the most expensive drug is the one that doesn't work, but it's equally true—if not more so—that the most costly drugs are the ones that aren't taken at all, or are taken incorrectly. The most carefully designed pharmaceutical benefits program in the world won't compensate for excessive *noncompliance*. This term applies to physicians who don't prescribe from a managed care plan's formulary or follow disease state management (DSM) treatment protocols and drug utilization review (DUR) guidelines. It also refers to patients who don't take prescribed drugs or take them so improperly that it interferes with their treatment and recovery.

Chapter 7...

Patient and Provider Compliance

The rising cost of prescription drugs and the high cost of noncompliance in both human and economic terms put a premium on making sure that medications are prescribed and dispensed only when appropriate and necessary, then taken by patients as directed. Drug-related problems that contribute to noncompliance can occur when an individual:

❍ Has a medical condition requiring long-term therapy but the appropriate medication is not prescribed
❍ Is taking the wrong drug for a particular illness
❍ Is taking too much or too little of a medication
❍ Is taking medication on a dosing schedule that results in an adverse reaction
❍ Stops taking medication because of side effects but fails to discuss the problem with a physician or pharmacist
❍ Is taking a drug that is not necessary.

Patient noncompliance with drug regimens costs the health plan twice, once for the medication itself, then again because more medication or more intensive medical care may be necessary as a result of the failure to comply. According to a study by the National Council on Patient Information and Education (NCPIE), "the economic consequences [of noncompliance] . . . include repeat physician visits, additional medications and therapies, specialist consultations, surgical procedures, and hospital stays. Indirect costs to employers include reduced productivity, absence from work, disability, and premature death."[1]

The extent and cost of noncompliance are astronomical. The annual total cost of patient noncompliance is estimated at more than $100 billion. Each year, noncompliance is linked to approximately $25 billion in hospital admissions, $5 billion in nursing home admissions and more than $50 billion in lost productivity.[2] Results of one study showed that approximately 10% of all elderly medical admissions were related to noncompliance, which cost $2,150 per admission.[3] Deaths from noncompliance with cardiovascular medications alone are estimated to total 125,000 per year.[4] One study concluded that hospitalization as a result of noncompliance accounts for more than 5% of all hospital admissions each year.[5]

Patient Noncompliance

One factor contributing heavily to the increase in patient noncompliance is the trend toward outpatient care. In the hospital environment, health care providers (primarily doctors and nurses) have substantial control over the administration of drugs. Ideally, the right drug in the right amount is given to the right patient at the right time via the right route.

Compliance is facilitated by such factors as these: related services such as medical, dietary and pharmacy are coordinated; each patient's record is kept on an individual chart; patient compliance with drug therapy is virtually mandatory; and therapeutic results and any adverse reactions are observed and monitored.

But when patients are on their own and medication administration is self-managed, it's a different story. Most of the time, no one is monitoring the patient to make sure he or she is taking the medication properly, or observing the patient to watch for side effects or determine if the medication is working. In addition, no one is checking to see that the medication is being stored and administered properly and is not being used by others.

One estimate states that approximately 7% of patients never even have their prescriptions filled after visiting a doctor.[6] A survey conducted by the American Association of Retired Persons (AARP) detailed a number of reasons that patients fail to fill prescriptions.[7] The major reason given was that patients didn't think the prescribed medication would help their condition. Concern about side effects came in a close second, and feeling that their condition had improved and drug treatment was not necessary was cited by one-fifth of those responding.

> *Cost is a significant factor in noncompliance, especially among older people.*

Cost is a significant factor in some noncompliance, especially among older patients, whose medications are not covered by Medicare except when they're hospitalized. Patients may not fill or refill prescriptions, take only a partial dose to stretch their supply of the drug and share medication with others in an effort to save money. Confusion and negative information about drugs that patients had heard or read about were also mentioned. According to one expert,[8] more than 90% of these problems reflect faulty communications between physicians and patients. Either doctors did not give patients all the information needed, or patients failed to ask their doctors the appropriate questions, or both. Elderly patients, especially those with failing eyesight, poor mobility or diminished mental capabilities, are sometimes confused about how medication should be taken, and verbal instructions from physicians or pharmacists are forgotten. Patients often stop taking medication when they start to feel better, too, not realizing that most prescriptions need to be finished to be fully effective. According to the AARP survey, 15% of patients stop taking their medication before the prescription runs out, and 32% don't obtain prescription refills as directed.

Several other factors may contribute to patient noncompliance with drug therapy. A complex medication regimen can be difficult to manage, especially for older patients. One study documented a direct relationship between the use of numerous medications and the number of hospital admissions resulting from noncompliance. Patients who were prescribed three or more medications had a higher rate of admissions related to noncompliance than those who took only one or two medications (9.8% versus 2.2%).[9] Also, patients who used multiple physicians and pharmacies without any centralized system of medication management were more likely not to follow directions accurately and have adverse reactions to drugs. Compliance has also been shown to decrease when there are long periods of time between doctor visits. Studies have demonstrated, too, that certain classes of medication, such as those used to treat respiratory diseases, are more likely to be associated with noncompliance.[10]

Physician Noncompliance

Patients aren't the only ones guilty of occasional—or habitual—noncompliance. Physicians may not achieve the objectives of optimal drug therapy when they:

◕ Do not prescribe the most effective drug
◕ Do not prescribe from the health plan's formulary
◕ Prescribe an inappropriate dose or quantity
◕ Prescribe drugs harmful to patients (due to adverse reactions and interactions with other drugs, allergies, potential for abuse or addiction, etc.).

Drug utilization review is the most effective tool to identify and control physician noncompliance and errors.

Drug utilization review (DUR), discussed in detail in Chapter 5, is the most effective tool used to identify and control physician noncompliance and errors. Mechanisms such as formularies, generic substitutions, step therapy and therapeutic substitution all encourage (or actually require) physician compliance. Retrospective and concurrent DUR monitors patterns of prescribing and dispensing. At the point of service, pharmacists use an online system (when available) to screen for: duplicate prescriptions, correct dosages, drug interactions, allergies, excessive refills and formulary compliance. One study of the consequences of pharmacist review found that detecting errors and preventing potential problems saved $2 per prescription.[11]

Influences and Strategies in Physician Noncompliance

Research discussed in the pharmaceutical literature indicates that there are five types of influence on physician behavior:

- Policy and administrative directives
- Economic
- Educational
- Patient directed
- Personal.

Research also shows that nine strategies have been shown to be most effective in influencing physician behavior:

- Classic continuing medical education (CME)
- Targeted CME
- Academic detailing
- Feedback (utilizing review mechanisms)
- Socioprofessional influences (published articles and peer opinion)
- Clinical decision support materials (algorithms, detail pieces)
- Patient education material (made available to physicians)
- Patient-centered influence (having patients request particular drugs or therapies)
- Administrative policy (formularies, rewards for compliance).

The most successful strategies are combinations of the above approaches, especially targeted CME coupled with academic detailing, clinical support materials and patient education materials.

Education: The Basis for Compliance

Education is the most logical and effective foundation for encouraging both patient and provider compliance. Educational efforts directed at both audiences are closely tied to the activities such as formularies, practice guidelines, disease state management and drug utilization review already discussed in previous chapters of this book.

In general, an education program is designed for one or both of these purposes: (1) to disseminate information and increase awareness and knowledge, and (2) to change attitudes and behaviors. The behaviors an MCO might want to change could include health-related decisions made by its members (smoking, overeating, etc.) and the clinical choices of health care professionals (in particular, drug therapy decisions made by physicians and pharmacists). Undesirable or problem behaviors—those that could negatively affect the quality or cost of patient care—become the target of educational compliance programs.

> *Educational programs are designed to increase awareness and understanding of a particular issue, change attitudes and behaviors, or both.*

Unfortunately, just acquiring new information does not necessarily result in the adoption of desired behaviors. Information may be a necessary prerequisite for changing behaviors, but it alone is usually not sufficient to cause change to occur. Examples of this include smokers who know the risks of smoking but continue to smoke, and patients who choose not to take necessary or helpful medication even after counseling by pharmacists or physicians. The gap between knowledge and behavior is also seen with providers when patient care decisions are made outside the parameters of current clinical knowledge.

Generally, PBMs in loosely integrated health care systems find that regulatory or administrative sanctions that encourage physician compliance are difficult if not impossible to enforce. Therefore, education programs are critical in encouraging providers, as well as patients, to comply with formularies, guidelines and DSM protocols. The key, however, is to first understand the factors and rationale underlying current behaviors in order to design the most relevant and appropriate program to disseminate information that will make lasting changes in behavior.

Desirable Program Characteristics

Changing the behaviors of patients and prescribers is a difficult task that requires more than simply providing information or making suggestions. Following are some characteristics of an ideal education program aimed at compliance control:[12]

- *The program is relevant.* Adults learn what they believe is necessary to solve their problems or perform better in their jobs. Assessing the current knowledge and motivation of a particular group of learners is essential for the program to be relevant to participants.
- *Program objectives are clearly defined.* A good education program must have explicit, measurable objectives.
- *The program is targeted to a specific audience.* For instance, high-volume or inappropriate prescribers, or high-risk patients and those with long-term illnesses, may be logical target audiences.
- *The program and its contents must be perceived as credible and believable.* One way to establish credibility is to use authoritative and unbiased sources of information such as published medical literature.
- *The program is characterized by active, participatory learning.* Activities might include discussion questions, case studies and problem-solving exercises.
- *The program should present both sides of an issue.* This can ac-

complish two objectives: (1) to enhance the credibility of the message, and (2) to stimulate active learning and participation.

❍ *The message should be vivid, capture the learner's attention and be easily recalled.* One-on-one visits and concise, concrete graphics are effective and memorable.

❍ *The program should include plenty of repetition and positive reinforcement of improved behavior.* Education programs should be ongoing, with frequent repetition of the message.

❍ *The program must have an evaluation plan* to assess whether objectives have been accomplished or a different strategy is called for. A good DUR program can provide data to assess changes in behavior. In general, an education program should be evaluated in terms of its impact on knowledge, attitudes and/or behavior. Then, questions like these should be asked: Does the target audience now know more about the subject? Have their attitudes changed? In what demonstrable ways have their behaviors changed? How has patient compliance been affected by an education program? How have prescribing patterns been impacted by a provider education program?

Program Content

The content of compliance-based PBM education programs is usually focused on a particular aspect of the plan's formulary, DSM program or other element of therapy management. The content may be tailored to plan members generally, patients with a particular disease, physicians or other prescribers, or pharmacists. Some examples of possible topics are:

❍ Information related to the prevention or early detection of a disease
❍ Recommended first line therapies
❍ Prescribing guidelines indicating how and when a particular drug or drug regimen should be used
❍ Auxiliary techniques that can enhance therapy (counseling, exercise, diet, etc.)
❍ Lifestyle changes that can prevent or minimize disease and enhance therapy
❍ Procedures and techniques for monitoring the effects of therapy
❍ Signs and symptoms of the illness itself and/or side effects
❍ What to do if side effects occur.

The results of an audit or drug use review may also become the subject of an education program. Here the content would be actual performance and alternatives to current undesirable behavior or reinforcement of desired behaviors. These are referred to *as audit-with-feedback programs.* In reporting performance data, participants might be presented with:

1. Aggregate results for the peer group or locale
2. Performance of the individual as compared to the performance of peers
3. Performance of the individual as compared to a quality criterion.

The data is disseminated in a variety of ways (e.g., printed material, group meeting, one-on-one visit, personal letter or phone call). Audit-with-feedback programs can be effective in changing physicians' prescribing behavior, especially when there are financial incentives to comply.

Delivering the Message

Compliance-based education programs are typically delivered in one, two or all of the following ways: (1) newsletters, printed materials, and audio- and videotapes; (2) group lectures and seminars; and (3) one-on-one visits (also called *academic detailing*). Each of these methods can be used with any topic and with audiences of patients, providers or both. While academic detailing is usually limited to physicians, a PBM can have dispensing pharmacists provide patients with information about their disease, treatment and appropriate drug therapy.

Newsletters and other printed material have not been shown to have a lot of influence in changing prescribing behaviors, but providing data or feedback about an *individual* physician's prescribing performance is more likely to be effective because it's more immediate and personalized. Printed material is often more effective with patients than it is with providers in increasing awareness and knowledge about a particular topic.

Lectures and seminars are often used with physicians (and infrequently with groups of patients), yet surprisingly little is known about their effectiveness in changing the prescribing behaviors of individual doctors or groups of physicians.[13]

Academic detailing, or one-on-one visits, is most often used with *outlier* physicians, or those whose prescribing patterns are outside the norm. This usually involves a representative of the PBM or health plan, such as a pharmacist or physician, who visits the prescriber in person. (Variations of the personal visit are phone calls and letters, which are sometimes used in the DUR process to alert providers to problems with their prescribing habits or with a particular patient's therapy.) Academic detailing is similar to *counterdetailing*, personal sales calls conducted by pharmaceutical company representatives, where the visitor explains the rationale for a particular therapy issue or drug choice and tries to convince the provider to change his or her behavior accordingly. The message is often reinforced with followup phone calls or printed material.

Industry Participants in Changing Plan Member Behavior

Managed care plans are in an excellent position to use patient compliance programs because of their emphasis on continuity of care, comprehensive patient records, and emphasis on wellness and prevention. Drug manufacturers, for their part, can encourage compliance by designing consumer-friendly packaging, single daily dose regimens and high-quality patient education materials.

Aside from the educational aspect of compliance programs, both patients and providers can be persuaded to change behaviors through financial incentives. With patients, these take the form of differential copayments and deductibles that save them money when they select the desired formulary drug product or way of obtaining prescriptions (e.g., mail order). For physicians, financial incentives take the form of positive reimbursement alternatives that allow them to earn more money when they comply with prescribing guidelines, such as choosing formulary drugs or following DSM guidelines and treatment protocols. On the negative side, noncompliant physicians may not share in leftover money in the plan's risk pool at year's end.

Both patients and providers can be persuaded to change behaviors through the use of financial incentives.

Monitoring Compliance

The effectiveness of compliance programs is typically monitored through the plan's drug use review system and its provider and/or patient profiles. DUR programs can also detect problems that may warrant additional educational interventions. In essence, DUR and education programs should be used together in most cases. First, DUR can identify problem behaviors among providers, patients or both; then education programs are designed to address and solve those problems; and finally, DUR data is used to evaluate the effects of the education program. (See Chapter 5 for a complete discussion of DUR.)

Questions to Ask About Patient and Provider Compliance

1. What is your philosophy about encouraging/requiring compliance with the drug program among prescribers? Among patients?

2. What provider education programs have been offered recently? What patient education programs? For each program:
   ◑ Who was the target audience?
   ◑ What was the rationale or purpose of the program? Was it related to DUR, DSM, formulary compliance or other PBM activity?
   ◑ What were the program's learning or behavioral objectives? Were these objectives based on an assessment of current knowledge or attitudes?
   ◑ What types of delivery were used (printed materials, lectures, seminars, one-on-one visits, etc.)?
   ◑ Was the message repeated, using multiple types of delivery?
   ◑ Was the program evaluated in terms of impact on behaviors? How? What were the results?

3. What resources are available for one-on-one compliance contacts? Are they made to prescribers, patients or both? Who conducts these visits? Are visits in person? By personal letter? By phone?

4. Is a regular newsletter published? For prescribers? For patients? For pharmacists?

Endnotes

1. "Misused or Unused Prescriptions May Cost Your Health Plan Plenty," *Business & Health Special Report: The Value of Pharmaceuticals*, 1991, 17.

2. R. A. Levy, "Noncompliance With Medication Regimens: An Economic Tragedy," *Emerging Issues in Pharmaceutical Cost Containment*, vol. 2 (Reston, VA: National Pharmaceutical Council, 1992), 1-16.

3. R. Brychell, "The Pharmacist's Role in Reducing Patient Noncompliance," *Medical Interface*, January 1993, 57.

4. R. L. Haskitt, "Patient Compliance: Tapping Into a Billion Dollar Drug Market," *Pharmaceutical Executive* 9 (7)(1989): 45-52.

5. J. D. Sullivan, D. H. Kreling and T. K. Hazlet, "Education Regimens and Subsequent Hospitalizations: A Literature Analysis and Cost of Hospitalization Estimate," *Journal of Research in Pharmaceutical Economics* 2(2)(1990): 1931.

6. J. Bender, "The Managed Care Prescription Benefit: Challenged by Shifting Care and Shifting Costs," *AAPPO Journal* 1(4)(1991): 11-18.

7. "Noncompliance With Medication Regimens: An Economic Tragedy," 1-4.

8. J. Heenan, "Prescription Drug Benefits in a Managed Care Plan: Balancing Quality and Costs," *Medical Interface*, January 1994, 91.

9. R. Brychell, "The Pharmacist's Role in Reducing Patient Noncompliance," 57.

10. Ibid.

11. "Prescription Drug Benefits in a Managed Care Plan," 88.

12. S. B. Soumerai and J. Avorn, "Principles of Educational Outreach to Improve Clinical Decision Making," *Journal of the American Medical Association* 263 (1990): 549-556.

13. S. B. Soumerai, T. J. McLaughlin and J. Avorn, "Improving Drug Prescribing in Primary Care: A Critical Analysis of the Experimental Literature," *Milbank Quarterly* 67 (1989): 268-317.

One of the most basic but critical decisions you must make is whether to handle your company's prescription drug benefits yourself as part of the total health care benefits package or contract with a PBM (pharmacy benefits management) company to administer them for you as a separate managed care program. As prescription drug costs have risen, there has been a strong trend in recent years toward contracting with a PBM to "carve out" a separate drug benefits program in an effort to control costs while maintaining or (ideally) enhancing quality.

PBM companies began proliferating in the early to mid-1990s because employers were disappointed to find that a piecemeal, "one-shot" approach to pharmacy benefits management just didn't work in controlling costs while still providing plan members with quality prescription services. In other words, expecting a single mechanism like a rebate program or a new network of pharmacies to be the "magic bullet" that would solve a company's problems with drug benefits was neither realistic nor effective. The widespread need for a more comprehensive, coordinated approach gave birth to the currently booming PBM industry.

Chapter 8...

Evaluating and Selecting a Pharmacy Benefits Management Company

According to Foster Higgins, the use of separately managed prescription drug programs, which had been growing steadily for several years, more than doubled in 1994. Close to half (44%) of large employers (500 or more employees) offered a separate prescription drug plan (in most cases, both a mail-order and card plan) in 1994. Three-fourths of these plans included online drug utilization review (DUR). The average cost was $405 per employee (up from $365 in 1993) and $595 per retiree.[1] Among very large companies with 20,000 or more employees, the percentage offering prescription drug card plans jumped from 36% to 66% in 1994.[2]

Unified Versus Carve-Out Plans

> *The trend in recent years has been to "carve out" prescription drug benefits and create a separately designed and managed program.*

When prescription drug benefits are part of the general health care package, some experts use the term *unified* to reflect their integration with other benefits, as opposed to being designed and administered separately. With unified pharmacy benefits, plan members submit paper claims and are reimbursed in the same way as for other medical services.

According to conclusions drawn by the Midwest Business Group on Health (MBGH), *unified pharmacy benefits* have the following advantages and disadvantages.[3]

Unified Pharmacy Benefit Advantages

- Administration is simplified for both the employer and claims payer.
- It's easier to coordinate benefits and combine the drug/medical deductible.

Unified Pharmacy Benefit Disadvantages

- The plan doesn't benefit from a preferred pricing structure, so plan members pay usual and customary (U&C) prices, which are higher than discounted prices available through most managed plans.
- Drug formulary and rebate arrangements are not possible.
- The claims payer lacks authority and flexibility and is usually unable to: adjudicate plan limitations and exclusions; enforce generic dispensing mandates; validate appropriate drug pricing by matching with average wholesale price (AWP); and may, in some cases, pay for drugs not actually covered due to a unified plan's lack of exclusionary protection.
- Claims paperwork provides little information except what's contained in copies of pharmacy receipts.
- Utilization and cost reports to plan sponsors provide minimal data beyond the number of claims processed and include no information on distribution and cost.

○ If there is a mail-order component, sufficient information is often not available to analyze plan experience as well as increases or decreases in costs.

○ Concurrent, retrospective and prospective drug utilization reviews are not feasible.

○ Drug benefit costs in a traditional major medical environment may be quite a bit higher than in a separately managed plan.

Because of a lack of flexibility and cost controls, the above disadvantages illustrate why many employers are choosing to separate, or *carve out*, their prescription benefits in order to better analyze and control expenses in this increasingly complex area. The term *carve-out* indicates that administration and management are handled by a specialized pharmacy benefits management (PBM) company, or administered by a more traditional insurer or third party administrator (TPA). The MBGH suggests that pharmacy carve-outs have the following advantages and disadvantages.[4]

> *Carved-out pharmaceutical benefits provide flexibility, control and an array of managed care options.*

Pharmacy Carve-Out Advantages

○ PBMs have the flexibility to design either a separate pharmaceutical deductible or one that's combined with medical benefits, depending on employer needs.

○ It's possible to access point-of-service (POS) benefit validation, eligibility verification, pricing information and claims submission data when drug benefits are separate.

○ A mail-order program can be integrated with retail pharmacy service so that such issues as employee communications and utilization/cost reporting are coordinated.

○ Various plan member cost-sharing arrangements are possible.

○ Carve-outs offer flexibility from one end of the spectrum to the other in terms of payment to the pharmacy. For example, members may be required to pay the full cost of the drug to their pharmacy and submit paper claims for reimbursement or, conversely, pay a $5 copay per prescription, with the pharmacy's POS system handling claims processing automatically.

○ PBMs typically support maximum allowable cost (MAC) pricing (see Chapter 4), as well as drug utilization review (DUR), formularies and manufacturer rebate arrangements.

○ An increasing number of PBMs and other carve-out vendors are beginning to provide performance guarantees and accept limited risk for drug benefit costs against defined budgets.

○ PBMs can offer creative ways to work with prescribing physicians and patients to enhance appropriate utilization and compliance.

Pharmacy Carve-Out Disadvantages

○ In cases where prescription costs are part of the major medical deductible, an employer must pay two administrative service fees: one to the PBM for partial claims adjudication, and another to the medical carrier for claims reimbursement and reporting.

○ Paper processing can entail a high fee in addition to charges for point-of-service claims adjudication.

○ A carve-out plan typically pays *all* pharmaceutical claims (or most claims with a paper-based plan) because they're filed electronically. A traditional major medical paper-based plan, in contrast, may benefit from the higher incidence of claims that are never actually submitted by plan members (the "shoe box effect").

> *Many consultants believe that the majority of benefits managers should contract with a PBM to manage drug benefits rather than try to handle administration and claims processing in-house.*

Because prescription benefits have become so much more complicated in recent years, many consultants feel that the majority of benefits managers should contract with a PBM for some or all needed services and not attempt to design and administer a pharmaceutical benefits program in-house. The claims processing function alone is probably beyond the scope of the average size company to handle efficiently and effectively in-house. It may be wise to discuss your circumstances and needs with a consultant who either specializes in pharmacy benefits or is very familiar with them as you make this major decision. However, keep your own interests and agenda firmly in mind when dealing with prospective consultants (or anyone selling services). Be wary of being sold services you don't need or *could* handle in-house.

What Services Do PBMs Offer?

As discussed in Chapter 1, PBMs vary substantially in size, scope and sophistication, but they all operate in a fairly similar fashion. Basically, PBMs externally apply various managed care principles and procedures to pharmacy benefits to contain costs and improve quality. PBMs may take the form of specialized companies that are devoted exclusively to managing prescription drug benefits, or they may be associated with health maintenance organizations (HMOs), preferred provider organizations (PPOs) or third party administrators (TPAs).

Some of the services PBMs offer (either as an inclusive package, on a menu basis, or as a mix customized for a particular client) include:

- ◗ Contract price negotiations with drug companies for discounted fees or capitated rates
- ◗ Rebate contracting
- ◗ Development and management of preferred provider networks of pharmacies, either chains or independents
- ◗ Reimbursement of retail pharmacies for their services
- ◗ Drug formulary development and management
- ◗ Claims processing
- ◗ Drug utilization review (DUR): prospective, concurrent and/or retrospective
- ◗ Patient monitoring
- ◗ Generic substitution programs
- ◗ Therapeutic substitution programs
- ◗ Academic detailing programs (i.e., one-on-one visits to physicians)
- ◗ Mail-order drug services and processing
- ◗ Outcomes and pharmacoeconomic research.

Managed Healthcare magazine's 1995 *Directory of Pharmacy Benefits Management Companies* lists 81 PBM companies. They range in size from industry giants covering 56 million lives and handling 350 million prescriptions a year to small, specialized PBMs (such as those dealing, for example, with medication for just one chronic disease) with 7,000 lives and 80,000 prescriptions per year.

As noted in the introduction to PBMs in Chapter 1, a PBM differs from a TPA in that a PBM attempts to control expenses by intervening in how drugs are prescribed and used. A PBM may perform many of the same claims processing and price-oriented administrative functions as a TPA, but a PBM is additionally involved in clinical or drug use decisions and programs designed to influence prescribing. These include drug use review, formularies, prior authorization, prescribing guidelines and disease state management (DSM) protocols.

> *Like TPAs, PBMs may handle claims processing and other administrative functions, but they are also involved in decisions designed to influence prescribing and utilization.*

Why Has the PBM Industry Grown So Rapidly?

The pharmaceutical industry and allied businesses are participating more directly in the evolving health care delivery market than ever before. One expert gives three reasons for the recent dramatic growth in the PBM market:[5]

1. More corporate benefits managers and state program administrators are realizing that pharmacy benefits *can* be effectively managed. That realization has led to an increase in the number of members in prepaid or managed drug benefit plans.

2. New PBMs have entered the market in response to the needs (actual or perceived) of benefits managers with prescription drug cost problems.

3. State and federal health care reform initiatives and private enterprises involving integration continue to broaden the market demand for managed pharmacy benefits.

The key to choosing a PBM is to understand two things: your needs and expectations, and a PBM's specific capabilities.

The downside of the PBM industry's rapid growth is that some of the newer PBMs are experiencing problems with quality, customer service and inadequate infrastructure because they've been poorly planned and pulled together hastily in order to take advantage of the booming marketplace. These problems, unfortunately, are then passed along to their clients. Beware of very new PBMs without a proven track record.

The key to evaluating and choosing the most appropriate PBM for your company's needs is to carefully analyze and clearly understand two things: your company's needs and expectations, and a PBM's specific capabilities. Because the PBM industry is growing so dramatically, many employers are making the mistake of jumping on the PBM bandwagon without taking a good, hard look at what their own circumstances and goals regarding pharmacy benefits are, then matching identified objectives with the most appropriate PBM available. Define exactly what you want your pharmacy benefits program to do. Is your priority to control costs? Is quality most important to you, or accessibility? What is the prevailing attitude among your company's employees about their benefits? Is it one of entitlement? How are more managed (i.e., restrictive) benefits likely to be received by your plan members?

Should You Choose a PBM
Owned by a Pharmaceutical Company?

If you decide to contract with a pharmacy benefits management company to carve out and administer your pharmaceutical benefits, an important question of very recent origin comes into play. Beginning in the fall of 1993, some of the country's largest and most powerful drug companies have purchased major PBMs. SmithKline Beecham bought DPS (Diversified Pharmaceutical Services), Merck & Company bought Medco Containment Services and Eli Lilly acquired PCS. These highly publicized acquisitions set off a flurry of "merger mania" that continues at the time of this writing, with a lengthening list of pharmaceutical manufacturers either purchasing PBMs outright or developing alliances, affiliations and partnerships with one or several PBMs. Some companies, including Pfizer, Rhone-Poulenc Rorer Pharmaceuticals and Bristol-Myers Squibb, have elected to forge strong alliances (often based on DSM programs) with PBMs rather than buy them outright. Still others, like Pharmacia & Upjohn, Inc., have taken a different route and developed their own disease state management programs.

These arrangements have raised serious questions about the ability of PBMs owned by drug companies to remain unbiased and objective in managing pharmacy benefits and, specifically, selecting drugs for formulary inclusion. Critics say these acquisitions are being pursued largely to obtain data and increase product sales and market share, mainly through broader representation on PBM formularies. The affiliated drug companies and PBMs retort that their relationships create not compromised objectivity and financial gain but stability, expanded expertise, greater resources and value-added services for payers, providers and patients. The truth probably lies somewhere in the middle.

From the employers' perspective, there are some additional questions. Affiliated PBMs claim that these partnerships allow for lower per unit costs. Does using a drug company-owned PBM result in lower pharmacy benefits costs for payers? Or have PBMs sacrificed their objective management abilities because they're under pressure, however indirect or subtle, to promote greater use of their parent company's products?

At this point, there is very little data available to answer these questions because even the first acquisitions are just a few years old. Also, most PBMs have proprietary formularies, and certain client privacy and confidentiality issues are involved. However, some consultants express concern and caution about PBMs owned by or affiliated with drug companies and advise payers to take a "let the buyer beware" attitude.

> *Have PBMs owned by large pharmaceutical companies compromised their objectivity to increase product sales, or have they expanded their expertise, resources and value-added services to the benefit of payers, providers and patients?*

One pharmaceutical benefits consultant stated that compromised objectivity *is* a legitimate concern, and that another problem with the larger affiliated PBMs is their "one size fits all" approach to benefits. This standardization translates into an inability to tailor a PBM program to the needs of client companies, especially smaller employers.[6]

However, large, multistate employers may be best served by a PBM owned by a pharmaceutical company because, among other advantages, they can negotiate better volume pricing programs and rebates.

There are several "red flags" to watch for in considering working with a PBM owned by a manufacturer.[7] Beware of PBMs touting huge rebates. This may indicate that plan sponsors are spending too much money on high-priced drugs. According to one expert,[8] manufacturers give rebates when they become concerned about losing market share, which often happens when a brand-name drug goes "off patent" and a less expensive generic product becomes available. Generic manufacturers rarely offer rebates because their products are lower priced to begin with, so if a drug company is giving big rebates on single source products, it may mean that plan sponsors are unnecessarily spending more money in the first place.

Another area to watch is therapeutic substitution programs, in which a product known to have the same therapeutic effect is substituted for another, usually in the interest of cost savings. Though therapeutic substitution is often legitimate and advisable, manufacturer-owned PBMs could use the practice to increase utilization of the parent drug company's products. Be cautious about what products are switched and examine the motivation behind the change. This requires either some research and education on the benefit manager's part or the advice of a consultant knowledgeable about specific drug products and therapeutic efficacy.

Finally, learn about edits and your authority and flexibility concerning them. Edits are special instructions for the pharmacist, patient or physician that are transmitted via computer as part of a pharmacy's point-of-service technology when a prescription is being filled. The pharmacist enters claims data into the computer, and within seconds the PBM transmits any edits that are appropriate as well as eligibility and copayment information.

According to one expert,[9] edits can be an important component in controlling utilization, especially in terms of the frequency with which certain drugs are prescribed. They can point out overlaps in drug therapy, control premature refills and warn of potentially dangerous interactions. The more frequent and instructive the edits, the more likely they are to be followed by the pharmacist. On the other hand, a PBM owned by a drug manufacturer may have its own agenda in promoting the prescription of particular products and therefore may be less inclined to control utilization, at least of its own drugs.

Large employers might want to consider contracting with several PBMs for different functions (claims processing, pharmacy network development and management, formulary, claims review, etc.). In effect, this would set up a system of checks

> *Though it may be more expensive, larger employers may want to consider using several PBMs for different services to ensure a system of checks and balances.*

and balances so that one PBM isn't responsible for every function, with the potential ability to manipulate data, reporting to the client only the most favorable information. Hiring several PBMs, though, can be more expensive, and you'd also want to ensure that the PBM companies were able to integrate their data.

How Are PBMs Paid?

A PBM is typically paid by an employer or employer group in one of three ways: (1) fee for service (so much per claim), (2) capitation (so much prepaid per member per month, *without* risk-sharing), or (3) capitation *with* risk.

The first generation PBMs (which organized networks, issued eligibility cards and processed claims but did little utilization management) were typically paid on a

> *PBMs are paid in one of three ways: fee for service, capitation or capitation with risk.*

fee-for-service basis. In other words, the PBM received a certain amount of money for each claim that was processed and paid but received no payment for its services if a claim was rejected. This arrangement avoided the incentive for an administrator to reject a claim for little reason, then approve it upon resubmission in order to receive two fees for the transaction. Ultimately, the employer paid the PBM a combination of the total paid to pharmacies for prescriptions and the fees for its services.

A more recent and currently popular payment method is *capitation*, where payment is a specified amount per enrollee, per time period. This payment is usually expressed in terms of per member per month (PMPM).

Capitation rates are based on drug utilization data, demographics and other factors that attempt to balance risk and reward for both the payer and the PBM.

The capitation amount might cover just the PBM's services or it might encompass all pharmacy benefit expenses, including payments to pharmacies for dispensing fees and ingredient costs. When capitation covers just PBM services, the employer bears the financial risk associated with the utilization of the benefit, while in the latter (described below), the PBM may share some of the financial risk.

As the pharmacy benefits manager becomes more actively involved in the prescription drug use process, a logical step in the reimbursement evolution process is for the PBM to assume some of the financial risk for the *total* cost of the benefit. With this arrangement, the payment to the pharmacy for prescriptions becomes the responsibility of the PBM and is not passed on to the employer, who therefore is not at risk. The capitation amount the PBM is paid covers its services as well as the benefit expenses, or a portion of that amount if the amount exceeds the agreed-upon capitated ceiling. The PBM stands to either gain or lose financially, depending entirely on the extent of benefit utilization. When this risk is shared by the PBM and the employer, neither party is totally responsible for the cost of services covered by the benefit.

Another aspect of risk-sharing is illustrated by situations in which PBMs share risk with pharmaceutical companies. This arrangement usually focuses on the shared management of disease categories. For instance, assume that a managed care plan expects a certain drug class used to treat a chronic disease to cost x dollars for a particular patient population. If the manufacturer's drug is used and costs *less* than anticipated, the PBM and manufacturer share in the financial rewards; but, if costs exceed expectations, the PBM must share expenses and/or penalties.[10]

With such direct financial arrangements, one might expect a capitated or otherwise at-risk PBM to be more actively involved in utilization control than it might be under an agreement where it has little or nothing to lose financially. The issue of financial risk is critical, in that it may affect the relationship between a PBM and its network pharmacies, where utilization takes place. To illustrate, two scenarios are possible. In one, the PBM seeks the least expensive methods of drug distribution. In the other, the PBM becomes more closely aligned with its participating pharmacies, expecting them to deliver predefined levels of service or pharmaceutical care (see Chapter 6). Pharmacies would complement the activities of the PBM by participating in organizational or networkwide activities to influence prescription drug use, such as formularies or prescribing guidelines. However, these functions are based on probability figures for large numbers of patients, even though drug therapy impacts individuals (positively and negatively) more than it does groups. The PBM can establish monitoring guidelines for network pharmacists, then track activities and capture data. This relationship could apply to other patient-specific services provided by pharmacists as well.

What Does It Cost to Manage Pharmacy Benefits Internally?

If you decide after analyzing your situation that it's best to manage your prescription drug benefits in-house, what will it cost, on average? According to one expert,[11] the administrative costs of an internal program vary greatly, but may be between $0.15 and $0.25 PMPM for the pharmacy services, with an additional $0.15 to $0.22 PMPM for claims processing. This can potentially yield between $2 and $3 PMPM in savings compared to fee for service, depending on the level of benefits offered and the extent of managed care strategies used during the first year.

The return from clinical programs in not as clear-cut. For example, it may cost $0.05 or more per claim when programs such as concurrent drug utilization review are implemented.[12] It's difficult to determine precise savings from various interventions into utilization and prescribing patterns. At any rate, the savings for any program generally will be greatest the first year, then go down as normal price and utilization increases result in an annual rise in the cost of continuing to provide pharmacy benefits.

In considering administering pharmacy benefits in-house, be clear on the costs involved for personnel, training and equipment. Cost savings from a managed prescription drug plan can easily be offset by the expense of handling functions (especially claims processing) internally.

Finding the Most Appropriate PBM

If you choose to engage outside help, it is probably wise to hire a consultant to help you identify which PBMs in your market would be the most appropriate for your needs, based on your corporate philosophy, demographics and need for particular services. Advice from other companies can be helpful as well, but bear in mind that they might not have made the best decisions, and the PBM industry is so young that few companies have much of a track record or a lot of research data yet.

Check with local managed care organizations and hospital purchasing alliances to see what pharmacy benefits consultants they have used successfully. The large national and international benefits consulting firms have pharmaceutical expertise, but so do much smaller firms. Costs range from a reasonable $100 an hour to tens of thousands of dollars for large projects with big name firms. Consultants charge for their services in different ways: an hourly fee, an estimated fee per project, a certain amount per plan member, or a monthly or yearly retainer. Interview several consultants and choose the one with whom you feel most comfortable and the one who has the clearest understanding of your needs.

> *Invest time in clearly defining your needs and objectives before considering PBM companies.*

Once you've selected a consultant, invest time in clearly defining your needs and objectives before proceeding on to consider PBM companies. These stated objectives are important not only in matching your company with the PBM best suited to help you but in evaluating the performance of a PBM, beginning about a year after you've started to work together. (See the end of this chapter for guidance on evaluating your PBM.)

Requesting Proposals or Information From Appropriate PBMs

There are several ways you can learn more about the specific services of those PBMs in your area that appear to be able to meet your needs. One is to engage a consultant to research, interview, evaluate and help you select the most suitable PBM. This consultant should start, as noted earlier, by sitting down with you to clearly identify your circumstances, problems, needs and objectives for a pharmacy benefits program. Once you both know exactly what services you need from a PBM, the consultant can select a number of specialized companies in your market who may be appropriate, then contact them, ask for information, conduct interviews and site visits, and narrow the list down to one or several PBMs best suited to you. With the consultant's input and recommendation, you can then meet with the candidates and work with your consultant to make a final decision.

The other PBM identification process involves putting out a traditional request for proposal (RFP) that asks interested PBMs to respond with specific information in a very structured format. RFPs are usually quite lengthy and time-consuming to complete. Recently, an alternative to RFPs, requests for information (RFIs), have become popular. These are typically shorter, less structured instruments that ask a number of

PBMs to answer specific questions such as those in the next section of this chapter. These answers are often submitted in writing, and those PBMs that appear to be qualified and attractive are invited for face-to-face interviews, either with you, if you're handling the process in-house, or your consultant if you've hired one to handle the selection and evaluation process for you. In either case, once you narrow down to the two or three best-qualified candidates, ask for client recommendations. One consultant recommends that you also ask about clients that have recently discontinued using the PBM, and why.[13]

If you decide to use an RFP or RFI, be aware that because of the way they're structured and the questions they ask, clever PBMs can turn them to their marketing advantage, using them as tools to present themselves in the best possible light by emphasizing their strengths and downplaying their shortcomings, problems or weaknesses in certain areas. Never make a decision based on claims made in an RFP alone. Interview candidates, discuss concerns at length, talk to references (preferably companies with demographics and needs similar to yours) and, when relevant, rely on your consultant's expertise and experience to choose the best PBM for you.

If you do decide to use an RFI, a very useful tool was jointly developed recently by the National Business Coalition on Health (NBCH), the Greater Detroit Area Health Council, Inc. and Pharmacia & Upjohn, Inc. The Managed Pharmaceutical Services Request for Information (RFI) Kit was specifically designed to guide individual employers and employer coalitions through the process of identifying, selecting and evaluating a PBM.[14] The kit is meant to provide a general framework and serve as a guide for employers putting out an RFI for a PBM for the first time. Its documents can easily be tailored to a company's individual needs. The kit begins with a suggested step-by-step time line for the whole process, with both aggressive and conservative time options. It gives a very specific structure for an RFI, addressing such elements as what the RFI requires of the PBM, a timetable, instructions for vendors' questions, price quotations based on different numbers of employees and information on site visits. An entire section is devoted to the main questionnaire, with questions asking for specifics on the following areas: vendor history, stability and qualifications; preferred pharmacy contracting; the pharmacy network; types of programs available; pricing; generics; member services; account services; information management and reporting capabilities; database(s); mail-order services; POS technology; formulary; DUR program(s); DSM program(s); and quality assurance.

The kit also provides a PBM evaluation tool (with an example) designed to offer structured suggestions for evaluating RFI responses. It provides a two-step decision making process that measures each PBM's response against preestablished criteria. Fill-in-the-blank charts are included. In addition, there are sample letters to potential PBM candidates, suggested questions for the face-to-face interviews, a contract outline and an RFI to use in seeking a pharmaceutical benefits consultant.

Questions to Ask in Selecting a PBM

Once you've identified the PBMs in your market that appear to be able to meet your needs, you'll want to find out exactly what their capabilities are so that you can compare them and select the most suitable candidate. Following are some categorized questions from *Managing Prescription Drug Benefits*[15] to ask during face-to-face meetings once you've narrowed the candidates down to two or three. (These questions take the place of the list that appears following most of the other chapters in this book.)

Networks

1. Can you administer a very limited network in our primary service area and a broader network elsewhere?

2a. Can you administer deductibles and percentage copayments in an on-line environment, integrating mail and retail?

 b. Can you administer deductibles as either stand alone or integrated with major medical?

3. Can you administer copayments as: percentage/fixed dollar/minimum dollar, separate mail/retail, generic/brand differential or pay only up to generic costs, preferred (formulary) and nonpreferred (nonformulary), in-network/out-of-network and/or annual stop-loss?

4. If you are not a mail-order vendor, what company do you expect to use? Can you integrate with a vendor of our choice? If so, are there additional fees involved?

5a. Do you perform onsite audits of retail pharmacies?

 b. Describe your audit process and indicate the number of pharmacies that you expect to audit in the next 12 months.

6. Describe your capabilities for both pharmacy and employee customer service (help desk). How do you measure their performance?

Claims Adjudication

1. Do you have 100% electronic claims adjudication capabilities?

2. Can you provide online eligibility verification as well as DUR and price data but also require paper claims for reimbursement?

3. In plans where paper claims are submitted, how do you measure claims adjudication performance? How frequently do you disburse checks? Where are paper claims processed?

4. How often are eligibility files updated? Can you provide eligibility edits online to our office?

5. What is your turnaround time for new ID cards?

Utilization Management and Reporting

1. What are the online edits you can provide?

2. Identify specific drugs or drug classes for which you recommend special limits or controls (for example, psychiatric drugs, high-cost/high-tech drugs, smoking cessation, Retin A, growth hormones, birth control pills, fertility drugs, DESI and injectables other than insulin).

3. How do you identify quality or cost-improvement opportunities with regard to: physicians, pharmacies, patients, products?

4. Specifically, how do you influence provider/prescriber behavior?

5. What data, tools, reports or other assistance can you offer that will help us monitor trends (prices, utilization, etc.) as well as your performance in managing the program?

Formulary and Rebate Management

1. Do you have a mechanism to collect manufacturer rebates for a program like ours? Describe it.

2. Do you utilize other forms of manufacturer assistance besides rebates? What are they?

3. Describe your recommendations for communicating formulary information to our employees and their physicians.

4. How frequently is your formulary reviewed and updated? As an example, describe which cardiovascular drugs are on your formulary and the process by which they are selected and periodically reviewed.

5. Will your formulary be modified to address any special characteristics of our employee/retiree population? Can the formulary be limited to just a few drug classes? Which ones would you recommend and why?

Prices

1a. What will retail network prices be for brand and generic drugs in our primary service area and elsewhere in the country?

b. Do you use maximum allowable cost (MAC) limits for multisource and generic drugs? How are these limits set?

c. Will we receive the lower of contract, usual and customary (U&C) or actual charges for drugs?

d. How will you share savings with us when you negotiate favorable prices?

2. What are your proposed mail-order prices for brand and generic drugs? Do you use a MAC list for mail order?

Fees

1. What are your fees for: network management, claims administration, utilization management and reporting, and formulary and rebate management? (Specify how the fees are structured: PMPM, per prescription or flat annual fee.)

2. Can you offer a capitated rate?

2a. What financial risk-sharing arrangements do you propose?

3. Do you suggest any performance guarantees, for example: generic substitution rates, formulary compliance, level of rebates, average cost per prescription, savings, employee satisfaction?

4. If you are also a mail-order service vendor, do your fees change if another company is the mail service provider?

5. Are there any additional administrative charges, such as for: claims versus prescriptions, transactions versus paid prescriptions, ID cards, employee materials?

Patient and Provider Compliance

1. Do you have patient and/or provider compliance programs in place? Describe them.

1a. What documented results have these programs had?

2. How you do participate in or suggest that employees be (1) educated about their pharmacy benefits and (2) trained to be more effective prescription drug consumers?

Legal Issues

Once you've selected the PBM that best meets your needs, you'll want to develop a legal agreement. Most PBMs have their own standard contract. Ask for a copy of it and have your company's legal department review and revise or customize it as appropriate. The PBM's legal counsel will want to be involved as well. Also, as noted earlier, the NBCH RFI Kit provides a very detailed standard contract format. Most contracts are for a one-, two- or three-year period, with a 90-day "out clause" applicable to both parties.

If you have been using a consultant up to this point in the evaluation and selection process, continue to seek your consultant's advice during the contracting phase. Your goal is to develop a contract that does the following: obligates the PBM to perform a very specific set of tasks and meet any agreed-upon performance guarantees (e.g., generic substitution rate, formulary compliance, rebate levels, average cost per prescription, savings, employee satisfaction); covers all contingencies that could reasonably be expected; and protects your financial and legal interests.

> *Your goal is to develop a contract that obligates the PBM to certain tasks and performance guarantees, covers contingencies, and protects your financial and legal interests.*

Evaluating Your PBM's Performance on an Ongoing Basis

After the first year of operation, enough data should have been accumulated to begin evaluating your PBM's performance. Rather than doing one evaluation at a certain time each year, experts recommend that, because functions are so intertwined and fluid, PBMs be monitored and evaluated on an ongoing basis throughout the year. Remember that there is typically a 90-day "lag time" from the point when a pharmaceutical transaction occurs until complete data on it are available.

According to one pharmaceutical benefits consultant with Towers Perrin, an international benefits consulting firm, your PBM should be judged throughout the year on how well it is performing in three key areas.[16]

Financial Results

Are your costs at the one-year mark and beyond in line with projections? Higher than expected costs are most often a result of poor utilization management. A review of the PBM's DUR programs and financial policies such as rebates and billing procedures should reveal whether its DUR program needs to be improved and, if so, whether the PBM is working toward making improvements.

Service Quality

Quality reviews should encompass not just the quality of specific services that the PBM provides to plan participants but broader issues such as patient confidentiality and product safety. How PBMs train their employees, fill orders and handle customer service is important. The Towers Perrin consultant notes that the following information should be examined: the number of PBM employees by job function and training (i.e., pharmacists versus support staff), number of clients served, number of prescriptions filled each year, and projected growth in claims and orders.

An evaluation should also ask the following performance-related quality questions:

- What procedures are in place for verifying patient eligibility for drug benefits, and who in the PBM can add or change eligibility information?
- What percentage of mail-order prescriptions handled by the PBM is actually checked and verified by more than one registered pharmacist?
- Under what circumstances are prescriptions referred to a consultant or pharmacist?
- What mechanisms are in place to handle situations in which a patient's prescription usage is suspect?
- In the past year, what percentage of prescription orders was reported lost in the mail?
- What safeguards are in place to prevent drug tampering, both within the PBM's facilities and after prescriptions have left the processing premises?
- What are the quality review procedures for generic drug substitution?
- What training and quality initiatives are in place to ensure that call-in patients receive accurate information and acceptable service from telephone service representatives?

Evaluate PBMs on how well they are performing in three areas: financial responsibility, service quality and responsiveness to your needs.

Responsiveness to Client Needs

This category concerns the PBM's relationship with you and your company and how responsive it is to meeting needs, addressing concerns and solving problems. Performance reviews should examine the quality of the PBM staff responsible for the employer's account and the extent to which it takes responsibility for client satisfaction. The quality of the PBM's information management system(s) is also important. The capabilities of the PBM's computer system, system interface and support personnel define its ability to accept employer-generated data, safeguard that data and generate reports.

When you begin to evaluate how well your PBM is working to meet your needs, you will realize the importance of having given it upfront a very specific list of tasks that it must perform to your satisfaction to keep your business. One consultant helps his clients develop a 15- to 18-item list of tasks when the PBM contract is developed; then that same list is used as a basis for evaluating the PBM's performance as time goes on. He stresses the importance of the evaluator's thorough understanding of pharmaceutical benefits management. The evaluator should either be the consultant or a company benefits manager who has been well educated by the consultant.[17]

> *Develop a list of task and objectives when you first contract with a PBM; then use the list as a basis for evaluating its performance.*

Data supplied by the PBM is typically organized into quarterly or semiannual reports, preferably by the consultant or benefits manager rather than the PBM. This eliminates the opportunity for the PBM to manipulate data and create reports that may not be completely objective and accurate. Costs for consultants to perform these evaluation services vary widely, depending on the scope and depth of services required (roughly between $1,000 and $10,000 per quarterly report).[18]

Think of an ongoing evaluation of your PBM's performance as protecting your financial investment in purchasing its services. Pharmaceutical benefits management has become a complex, multifaceted business. The majority of employers must rely on a PBM to handle the responsibility in an efficient, effective and coordinated fashion. An ongoing evaluation process is a kind of insurance policy in maintaining the trust you've placed in the PBM to do the best possible job of managing your pharmaceutical benefits.

Endnotes

1. "Employers Move to Value-Based Purchasing," Foster Higgins news release, May 31, 1995, 2.

2. "Employer Health Benefit Cost Drops in 1994," Foster Higgins news release, February 14, 1995, 2.

3. "Managing Prescription Drug Benefits" (Chicago: Midwest Business Group on Health, 1994), 20.

4. Ibid.

5. R. Navarro, "Competition Through Creativity," *Medical Interface*, June 1994, 62.

6. Telephone interview with Bill Pinter, R.Ph., Integrated Prescription Services, Troy, MI, July 20, 1995.

7. S. Peard, "Rx/PBM Mania Merger Is Bad for Plan Sponsors," *Employee Benefits News*, February 1995, 21.

8. Ibid.

9. Ibid., 22.

10. "Pharmaceutical Companies Share Risk in New Alliances," *Managed Care Selling Edge* (Boston: Total Learning Concepts, Inc., 1994), 3.

11. R. Navarro, "Justifying the Cost of Pharmacy's Clinical Services," *Medical Interface*, September 1994, 69-70.

12. Ibid.

13. Telephone interview with Bill Pinter, July 20, 1995.

14. To order or for more information, contact the National Business Coalition on Health (NBCH), 1015 18th St. NW, Suite 450, Washington, DC 20036; phone (202) 775-9300; fax (202) 775-1569.

15. R. Ekstrom, "Selecting a Pharmaceutical Benefits Manager," *Managing Prescription Drug Benefits* (Chicago: Midwest Business Group on Health, 1994), 22-24.

16. K. Babbin, "Performance Issues Loom Large in the Managed Pharmacy Industry," *Journal of Compensation and Benefits*, September-October 1994.

17. Telephone interview with Bill Pinter, July 20, 1995.

18. Ibid.

The future of prescription drug benefits will be like the present in at least one way: *Change* will be the one constant we can count on. Happily, the majority of the changes on the horizon should make your job as a benefits manager easier and your employees' drug benefits better in every way.

Following are some of the trends that impact pharmaceutical benefits now and that are expected to continue or gain strength into the 21st century.

❍ Health care will continue to be viewed on a continuum from prevention and early identification of illness through acute and chronic episodes of care. The systems approach will increasingly replace the component-based model of health care that has prevailed until recently. All types of medical services and pharmaceutical products will become more interrelated and integrated into the system as a whole.

❍ The trend toward mergers, alliances and other partnerships among managed care organizations, pharmaceutical manufacturers, PBMs and related businesses will continue. In the foreseeable future, there will be fewer but larger MCOs, manufacturers and PBMs as the current "urge to merge" moves steadily forward.

❍ Pharmaceutical products—and pharmacists—will play an increasingly important role in overall health care as evidence accumulates that drug therapy is often the least expensive form of treatment. Pharmacists will be better recognized as knowledgeable consultants to physicians, patients and health plans.

❍ As the American population continues to age

Afterword...

The Future of Pharmacy Benefits

and chronic diseases predominate, more prescriptions will be written than ever before. Most experts believe that formularies will shrink and become more selective and restrictive.

O Outcomes studies will more clearly define what works and what doesn't in medicine and drug therapy. Specialized outcomes research such as pharmacoeconomics will help meet providers' demands for data to support treatment and prescribing decisions and employer demands to support health care expenditures.

O Practice guidelines and other forms of universal treatment and prescribing protocols will be more numerous, and providers of all types will be forced to standardize care.

O To keep costs down, employers will find new ways to encourage employee wellness and disease prevention. Innoculation programs for both adults and children will grow, and a variety of initiatives and programs will give responsibility for health care management back to employees, asking them to be more accountable for their own health and share more of the benefits cost.

O Technology will continue to advance in amazing ways. The information highway is moving steadily toward linking and integrating all components of health care: MCOs, hospitals, physicians, pharmacies and PBMs. Sophisticated computer science will make possible a central repository of information on a patient's medical and prescription history, reports from all participating health care professionals, test results and benefits coverage.

O Eventually, handwritten prescriptions will become obsolete. Physicians, bound by stricter guidelines, will access DUR data online and enter prescriptions before transmitting them by computer to pharmacies. This will help prevent errors and inappropriate or needlessly expensive prescribing.

This is an exciting time for everyone involved in the pharmaceutical field as creative ways of thinking, new managed care strategies and technology make possible advances that were undreamed of just a few years ago. These changes should provide numerous clinical and financial advantages to both providers and patients. Employers and plan sponsors should find that innovations already underway—with more to come—will help them manage the cost, quality and accessibility of prescription drug benefits more efficiently and effectively than has been possible before.

AAC (Actual Acquisition Cost): the price a pharmacy actually pays for a drug.

Adjudication: the process of making claims payment decisions.

Adverse Drug Reaction (ADR): occurs when a particular drug is harmful to a patient.

Algorithms: a set of steps or protocols for a particular drug therapy.

Average Wholesale Price (AWP): the most common price a pharmacy would pay a wholesaler to buy a specific quantity of a drug.

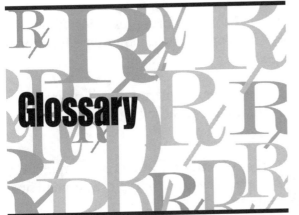

Glossary

Bioavailability: the rate and extent of a drug's absorption in the body.

Bioequivalent Drugs: drugs that have the same active ingredients, strength and dosage form.

Brand-Name Drug: a product for which a manufacturer has patent protection. Usually available from only one source.

Capitation: fixed amount paid to a provider in advance per member, regardless of the number or type of services subsequently used. Usually expressed as "per member per month" (PMPM).

Carve-Out: separately designed and administered benefit plan for particularly high-cost benefits (pharmacy, mental health, etc.).

Case Management: a process to contain costs and enhance quality of care that includes developing a coordinated plan of treatment for patients. Overseen by a case manager.

Compliance: patient adherence to a prescribed drug regimen or treatment plan, or provider adherence to health plan guidelines such as formulary, practice protocols, etc.

Cost Shifting: in pharmacy, the process by which drug manufacturers or providers give discounts to one sector, then pass the cost along to another sector.

DESI (Drug Efficacy Study Implementation) Drugs: drugs classified by the FDA in 1962 as safe but not proven fully effective by today's standards.

Detailing: a process by which drug experts inform prescribers about the cost and efficacy benefits of particular products, either for educational or sales purposes.

Distributive Services: delivery-related services performed by pharmacists including acquisition, storage, handling, repackaging, labeling and distribution.

DRR (Drug Regimen Review): type of drug utilization review to identify inappropriate or potentially harmful drug therapy. Typically used in hospitals and long-term care facilities.

Drug Misadventures: errors in ordering, transcribing, dispensing and administering drugs.

DSM (Disease State Management): comprehensive, integrated systems approach that targets costly, chronic diseases. Aims to control costs by using the most effective treatments as early as possible.

DUE (Drug Use Evaluation): quality assessment review of drug utilization.

DUR (Drug Utilization Review): system that monitors use and improves quality of prescription drug use in a health plan.

EAC (Estimated Acquisition Cost): discount off average wholesale price (AWP) that pharmacy benefits manager pays pharmacy (e.g., "AWP minus _____%").

EDI (Electronic Data Interchange): computer networks that link various providers, collecting and organizing pharmacy claims data for use in outcomes research.

Edits: instructions for pharmacists, patients or physicians transmitted electronically through point-of-service (POS) technology as prescription is being filled.

Fee for Service (FFS): traditional indemnity reimbursement method where patient pays for pharmaceutical or medical service upfront and files for reimbursement later. Providers are paid a fee for each service they deliver.

Formulary: health plan or hospital's list of approved or recommended drugs, with additional information. Those drugs deemed to be the most effective and economical.

Generic: bioequivalent, lower cost version of a brand-name drug, available when patent protection expires on a brand-name drug.

Generic Substitution: process of substituting a lower cost generic version of a brand-name drug, when available.

IHMDS (Integrated Health Management Delivery System): system to manage and measure behavior of patients and providers, with the goal of achieving optimum wellness through the most appropriate use of cost-effective products and services.

Legend Drugs: pharmaceutical products available only by prescription.

MAC (Maximum Allowable Cost) List: upper limit prices that health plan will reimburse for generic or multisource products.

"Me-Too" Drugs: drugs that are no better therapeutically than their predecessors in the same drug class.

Multisource: generic drugs available from multiple sources.

Off-Label: drug used for purposes other than those originally intended. Not approved for alternative uses by the FDA.

OTC (Over the Counter): pharmaceutical products available without a prescription.

Outlier: prescriber, drug use, etc., that falls outside an average, normal range. Often responsible for high costs.

PBM (Pharmacy Benefits Manager/Management): refers either to an individual or to a company that manages pharmacy benefits.

Pharmaceutical Care: wide range of pharmacist services (assessment, monitoring, education, etc.) that promote comprehensive, coordinated management of patients' medication use, with the goal of optimum outcomes. Related terms are **cognitive services**, **clinical pharmacist services** and **professional services**.

Pharmacoeconomics: a decision making tool for comparing and integrating costs and outcomes of drugs. Four most common types of analysis are: cost-benefit, cost-utility, cost-effectiveness and cost-avoidance.

Pharmacoepidemiology: science of detecting and preventing inappropriate prescribing, either on a patient population or individual physician basis.

Pharmacology: science dealing with the preparation, uses and effects of drugs.

Pharmacy Benefits Management: organizational activities designed to influence the behaviors of prescribers, pharmacists and patients to affect the cost and use of prescription drugs.

PMPM (Per Member Per Month): in a capitated health plan, indicates amount prepaid to provider for each subscriber, regardless of services actually used. Puts provider at financial risk.

POS (Point of Service): refers to computerized technology that allows pharmacists to electronically access and enter data in real time as prescriptions are being filled. Link between delivery system (retail or mail) and PBM that facilitates eligibility verification, claims adjudication and DUR.

Practice Guidelines: (Also known as **practice policies, treatment protocols** and **critical pathways**.) Recommendations issued in advance of the delivery of health care services designed to influence treatment or prescribing decisions.

Prescribers: health professionals permitted by law to prescribe medications. Includes physicians, nurse practitioners, dentists and (with some restrictions) may include optometrists, podiatrists and chiropractors. Pharmacists have limited prescribing authority in several states.

PSAO (Pharmacy Services Administration Organization): network of pharmacies or pharmacists that contract with employers, insurance carriers, third party administrators (TPAs) or pharmacy benefits management (PBM) companies to provide services for plan subscribers.

Rebate: program in which manufacturers pay the PBM a certain amount based on the quantity of their product(s) sold through the PBM.

RFP/RFI (Request for Proposal/Request for Information): two types of instruments used to solicit information from vendors interested in supplying a service (e.g., employer solicits information about services from PBM company).

Shoe Box Effect: in a fee-for-service system, some plan members accumulate pharmacy receipts but never actually get around to filing claims. Health plans make money when claims are not filed, versus managed systems where all claims are filed electronically when prescriptions are filled.

Single Source: term used when a drug can only be purchased from one source, usually the original manufacturer.

Step Therapy: (Also called stepped therapy.) In pharmacy, the practice of initially treating a patient with the least expensive drug or therapy, then moving to higher cost medications or therapies only if necessary.

Therapeutic Substitution: practice of substituting one drug for another (a **therapeutic alternate**) when both are thought to produce the same therapeutic effects.

Therapy Management: the process of defining and implementing a certain regimen for the management of a particular disease, in a systems context with integrated resources. Involves outcomes research, economic evaluation, treatment protocols, and provider and patient compliance.

U&C (Usual & Customary) Charges: the price a retail pharmacy charges customers who pay cash for a specific drug.

Unified Benefits: term used to indicate that all benefits are part of the general health care plan rather than any being separate or "carved out."

Accessibility of care, 17
see also Pharmacy benefit plan design

Benefits manager
role of, 1
Bioequivalent products *see* Generic substitution

Capitation *see* Pharmacy reimbursement
Carve-out plans
advantages of, 113-114
described, 113
disadvantages of, 114
see also Unified plans

Index

Claims processing
changes due to
computers, 39
methods of, 24
point-of-sale (POS)
electronic claims
technology, 39-40
role of pharmacy
benefits management
companies, 39-40
Communication
importance to pharmacy
benefit plans, 25
Cost-containment
as focus of managed care, 7-8
Cost-effectiveness
as consideration in drug therapy, 8
Counterdetailing, 73

Data collection
purposes of, 24
Delivery options for outpatient pharmacy services
closed network, 29
combination, 32
company pharmacies, 30

Long-term care pharmacists, 76
see also Drug regimen review
(DRR), Drug utilization
review (DUR)

Managed care
failings of component model,
83-84
increase in plan enrollment, 1-2
integrated system model, 84-85
role of pharmacy benefits in, 85
use of patient compliance
programs, 109
see also Outcomes research,
Pharmacy benefits manage-
ment (PBM) programs
Member cost-sharing
defined, 18-19
effects on costs and utilization,
19-20
incentives to use generic
products, 20-21
online adjudication through
point-of-sale system, 19
types of, 19
Member satisfaction, 17
importance of measuring, 43
see also Pharmacy benefit plan
design

Noncompliance
as problem in pharmacy benefits
management programs, 101
drug-related problems
that contribute to, 101
high cost of, 102
monitoring compliance, 109
use of financial incentives
to combat, 109

see also Education as basis
for compliance, Managed
care, Patient noncompliance,
Physician noncompliance

Omnibus Budget Reconciliation
Act of 1990 (OBRA '90) see
Drug regimen review (DRR),
Drug utilization review (DUR),
Pharmacy quality
Outcomes research
defined, 95
importance of, 95
need for more research
and meaningful data, 95
prevalence of outcomes
programs, 95-96
role of electronic data interchange (EDI) networks, 95
therapy management, 98
see also Pharmacoeconomics

Patient noncompliance
communication problems, 103
cost as factor, 103
difficulty of managing complex
medication regime, 103-104
failure to fill prescriptions, 103
role of outpatient care, 102-103
Pharmaceutical care
cognitive or professional
services, 85-86
described, 85
role in improving patient
outcomes, 86
two components of pharmacy
benefits, 85

Pharmacoeconomics
  described, 96-97
  four models commonly used, 97
  uses for, 97-98
Pharmacoepidemiology, 73
Pharmacy benefit plan design
  described, 15
  importance of, 15-16
  see also Effective pharmacy
    benefits, Efficiency of care
**Pharmacy benefits management
  (PBM) companies**
  differences from TPAs, 115
  downside of growth, 116
  proliferation in '90s, 111,
    114, 116
  issues related to pharmaceutical
    company ownership or
    affiliation, 117-119
  key to evaluating and choosing,
    116
  methods of payment, 119-121
  need for legal agreement, 127
  role of, 111
  services offered, 9-10, 114-115
  use of consultants in selection
    process, 121-122
  see also Evaluation of pharmacy
    benefits management (PBM)
    company, Selection of phar-
    macy benefits management
    (PBM) company
**Pharmacy benefits management
  (PBM) programs**
  cost of, 111-112
  definition of, 8
  evolution of, 10-11
  growth of, 111-112
  interventionist approach to
    drug use and prescribing, 12
  parties involved, 8-9

Pharmacy quality
  importance of monitoring
    for closed networks, 40
  OBRA '90 requirements
    for pharmacies serving
    Medicaid patients, 42
  three dimensions of, 41-42
Pharmacy reimbursement
  capitation, 34-36
  components of, 21-22
  direct pay, 11
  evolution of methods, 38-39
  incentive payments, 38
  maximum allowable cost
    (MAC), 33-34
  methods, 32-39
  payment for cognitive service, 38
  product cost plus fee, 32-33
  risk sharing, 36-37
  usual and customary (U&C)
    charges, 37-38
Physician noncompliance
  described, 104
  influences on physician
    behavior, 104-105
  role of drug utilization review
    (DUR), 104
  strategies for influencing
    physician behavior, 105
  see also Formularies
**Plan limitations, restrictions
  and exclusions**
  coverage limitations, 22-23
  drug efficacy study implementa-
    tion (DESI) drugs, 23
  experimental drugs, 23
  prior authorization programs, 24
  types, 22-23
  use of drugs for off-label
    indication, 23-24

*For more information on managed care topics, look to these books
also published by the International Foundation.*

◆ Managed Vision Benefits

by Jesse Rosenthal, O.D., M.P.H., and Mort Soroka, Ph.D.
This book is the first of its kind on managed vision care benefits. It is a must for benefits managers who wish to offer vision care as part of their employee benefits package. It provides an overview of managed vision care, the components of a standard vision benefits package, provider information, essential elements of a delivery system, and information on cost, quality and administration of plans. Of special interest is a directory of vision care plans and a sample summary plan description.
189 pages. 1995. ISBN 487-9. $37.

◆ Managed Dental Care: A Guide to Dental HMOs

by Donald S. Mayes, D.D.S.
Benefits managers can master the basics of dental benefits with the help of this book. This guide provides the information necessary in evaluating, selecting, purchasing and monitoring dental HMO plans. The author has reviewed dozens of plans and has identified the characteristics of those that are well designed, provide excellent value and offer quality dentistry, as well as a high level of satisfaction to purchasers, patients and participating dentists. The book outlines an expected mix of services and includes a checklist of good plan design and management, "tricks and traps" to look out for, a list of dental HMOs and key elements of a request for proposal.
248 pages. 1993. ISBN 464-X. $49.

◆ Mental Health Benefits—A Purchaser's Guide

by William M. Glazer, M.D., and Nancy N. Bell
Mental health benefits and substance abuse costs are a critical part of the total benefits picture. This book assists benefits managers in understanding and controlling mental health services and costs by providing information on the managed care approach to mental health benefits, mental health cost audits, psychiatric chemical dependency and psychiatric disorders masquerading as medical conditions. Checklists are included for a variety of topics, including issues to consider when choosing a vendor and how to evaluate a contract EAP.
206 pages. 1993. ISBN 459-3. $49.

To order these books, call toll free: **(888) 33-IFEBP.**